HOW TO DEBATE

REVISED EDITION

BY ROBERT E. DUNBAR

A SPEAK OUT, WRITE ON! BOOK
Franklin Watts
New York/Chicago/London/Toronto/Sydney

For my son, Jesse, who has argued himself
into a law degree

Material from *Firing Line* quoted on pp. 31–35, 47–49, 53–54, 61–62, 67–
69, is Copyright © 1990, 1991 by the Southern Educational
Communications Association, P.O. Box 5966, Columbia, S.C. 29250.
Copies of the complete transcript are available from SECA. Debate forms
in Chapter 9 are reprinted by permission of Wadsworth Publishing Co.

Photographs copyright ©: The Bettmann Archive: p. 9; Rothco Cartoons:
pp. 14 (Dick Adair), 20 (Mitro), 30 (Tom Gibb); Wide World Photos:
pp. 37, 72; Reuters/Bettmann: p. 73

Library of Congress Cataloging-in-Publication Data

Dunbar, Robert E. (Robert Everett)
How to debate / Robert E. Dunbar. — 2nd ed.
p.   cm. — (Speak out, write on! book)
Includes bibliographical references and index.
ISBN 0-531-11122-9
1. Debates and debating—Juvenile literature.   [1. Debates and
debating.]   I. Title.   II. Series.
PN4181.D86 1994
808.53—dc20   93-11959 CIP AP

ACKNOWLEDGMENTS

I am grateful to the following persons for their assistance and contributions to this new edition of *How to Debate*: Robert J. Hoy, Debate Coach, Brunswick High School, Brunswick, Maine; Scott Murray, student debater, Scarborough High School, Scarborough, Maine; and Nathan Dennis, a Citizen Judge representing Mt. Ararat High School, Topsham, Maine.

Dan Schwager and Sarah Watson, students at Bates College, Lewiston, Maine; Hajime Kawada of Waseda University and Tomoyuki Uda of Sophia University, Japan; participants in the International Debate held February 26, 1992, at Bates College.

Professor Scott Deatherage, Director of Debate, and Kevin Hamrick, Assistant Director, Department of Communication Studies, Northwestern University, Evanston, Illinois.

ONTENTS

ONE

THE JOYS AND CHALLENGES OF DEBATING

If you've never taken part in a debate before, you'll be surprised and pleased at the benefits this experience can bring you. Debating gives you the opportunity to develop poise and confidence in expressing your attitudes and opinions about any subject. You'll also be developing skills in the use of language that will serve you well throughout your life.

Debating is not an activity you can approach casually; however, you'll be well rewarded for whatever effort you put into it. You'll learn how to think for yourself, and how to think on your feet when challenged in a fair-minded discussion based on well-researched evidence to prove your points. Whether you are on the affirmative side (in favor) or the negative side (not in favor) of a controversial issue (called the "resolution" or "proposition" in formal debating), you will learn how to respect differences of opinion as well as how to present convincing arguments in support of your own point of view.

Debating is free of the passion of a shouting match or personal argument because you deal with facts and evidence, not emotions. You concentrate on convincing judges and audience to agree with your stand on a particular issue, based on your presentation of the facts and your conception of the good or evil of a situation or principle. There is also the enjoyment factor.

PERSONAL ENJOYMENT

As one debating teacher expressed it: "The first and most obvious benefit is personal enjoyment. A debater likes competitive debating. It's fun. Once you have taken part, once you have felt the thrill of matching wits with your opponents before an audience, no great sales effort is necessary to keep you interested."[1]

Debating is a common experience in democratic countries like the United States where everyone is free to express his or her opinion about anything under the sun. Every time there is an election, political candidates debate all the important issues in efforts to convince the public to vote for them. Any time there is a public controversy about any aspect of the human condition—the environment, freedom of speech and expression, education, morality, rights of privacy—proponents and dissidents come forth to discuss and debate both sides of the issue. That is one of the glories of living in a democracy.

MEMORABLE LANGUAGE

Debating can stimulate and inspire a person to use clear, concise, and memorable language. Americans have never forgotten some of the language Abraham Lincoln used in his debates with Stephen A. Douglas during the Illinois U.S. Senate campaign of 1858.

Although Lincoln lost that election, he later became president and commander-in-chief of the Union forces in the Civil War of 1861–65, which led to the resolution of the slavery issue. Scholars continue to study the

"Sit down, Lincoln, your time is up." This cartoon illustrates a scene during one of the Lincoln-Douglas debates. Douglas, who had been walking up and down on the platform with his watch in hand, finally called that time was up on Lincoln's argument.

Lincoln-Douglas debates not only because they provide such a rich and instructive storehouse of all the elements involved in debating, but because they were so important to the history of this country and its future development. The Lincoln-Douglas debates also led to a style and format of debating that has become especially popular in high school debating programs.

THINKING CLEARLY

One of the essentials of successful debating is thorough preparation. This means among other things that you must learn how to examine a question critically from both affirmative and negative points of view. Whatever terms you use in your arguments to prove your case, for or against, must be carefully defined. You must also learn how to sift the relevant arguments from the irrelevant. This gives you superb training and experience in how to think clearly about any issue.

RESPECTING THE OPINION OF OTHERS

Your primary goal as a debater is to be able to debate an issue so successfully and persuasively that you or your team will be judged the winner. To reach this goal you must learn how to master all the elements of debate. In essence, you must know how to find and present the most convincing arguments and evidence to support the side you represent. You must learn how to examine both sides of an issue thoroughly so you will be well prepared to respond to any argument or challenge by your opponents. As a debate progresses, you must have the ability to take important notes quickly when your opponents are speaking. In these ways you will be prepared to answer any argument they present when it's your turn to speak.

Regardless of the outcome of any debate in which

you participate, however, you will always be a winner if you learn to respect the opinions of others. Along with developing your powers of reasoning and argument and the ability to support your stand on a particular issue, that is one of the most important benefits of debating.

THE JOYS, CHALLENGES,
AND BENEFITS OF DEBATING

- Through development of research skills, learning how to examine a question or problem critically from both affirmative and negative points of view
- Learning how to judge the reasonableness and relative importance of arguments and evidence
- Development of language skills
- Learning how to think for yourself and how to think clearly
- Learning how to find the best arguments and evidence to support your point of view
- The opportunity to develop poise and confidence in expressing your opinions
- The fun of matching wits with opponents
- Learning to respect the opinions of others

TWO

HOW DEBATES ARE JUDGED

Whatever the format happens to be, judging a debate is a difficult task. In making a decision, a judge will consider certain basic elements, including the following:

1. The strengths and weaknesses of the arguments
2. How well the challenged arguments are answered
3. The errors in evidence and reasoning that are pointed out or ignored by either side
4. If an argument is dropped, missed, or not answered, whether or not this is called to the judge's attention by the opposing side (an important consideration in determining who has won the debate)[1]
5. The effectiveness of the delivery

In support of the decision as to which side was more effective in debating a proposition or resolution, the judge will take notes throughout the debate. There may be times when a judge is especially knowledgeable about the proposition being debated, but this knowledge must be put aside and not allowed to influence the judge's decision. Only the evidence and arguments that both sides have introduced must be considered. Even though some of the evidence may be superficial or incomplete (based on the judge's knowledge of the subject), the participants must be judged on *their* knowledge, not the judge's.

When weak evidence is introduced, it must be accepted at its face value. Throughout the debate the strengths and weaknesses of the arguments and evidence presented by both sides will be evaluated. Using the ballot provided, the judge will indicate this by assigning points for each phase of the debate as carefully and fairly as possible. When it is obvious that one side could have made a much stronger argument on a particular issue, the judge must note whether the opposing side countered or challenged that particular argument. Any time one side does not answer an argument presented by the opposing side, points will be deducted from its score.

Every debate must be judged within its own framework. For this reason, almost any statement made or position taken by either the affirmative or negative side will stand until denied by an opposing argument or evidence. Any errors of omission or failure to challenge an argument or evidence will be so noted. The quality of each debater's delivery is important, but even more important is how well he/she presents arguments and whether or not the arguments are carried through effectively throughout the debate round by both sides.

JUDGING POLICY DEBATE

A good way to understand how debaters are judged is to review the guidelines followed by judges in the more popular types of high school competition. One is the Policy Debate, also known as Oregon Style or Team

Debate, in which there are two debaters on each side of a resolution, affirmative and negative. In this style of debating the two members of the affirmative team argue in favor of the resolution and present a plan that must prove certain stock issues that form the basis for the resolution being debated.

For example, one recent resolution suggested by the National Forensic League was:

Resolved: That the Federal government should significantly increase social services to homeless individuals in the United States.

There may be four or five stock issues, depending on the guidelines set for a particular debate round. The four stock issues that must be proved in all Policy debates are:

1. significance
2. inherency

3. solvency, and
4. advantages. The fifth stock issue, if included, is
5. topicality.[2]

In proving the first stock issue—*significance*, or harms—the affirmative team must convince the judge that there is a *significant* problem with the present system, that the present system or status quo is bad. The affirmative team must not only declare the situation to be bad or harmful, however, it must explain why it is harmful and why it is a problem.

In proving the second stock issue, *inherency*, they must give convincing evidence that the problem is *inherent*, or central, to the present system. They must present evidence that the homeless are not receiving the help they need. The affirmative side must also show that a major change in policy, as advocated in their plan, is needed if the problem is going to be solved. The present system won't fix itself. If that were possible there would be no need for the affirmative's plan. They must also prove that a barrier exists which prevents the plan from going into effect or the problem from being solved.

This leads into the next stock issue, *solvency*. In proving this stock issue, the affirmative side must convince the judge that their plan will *solve* the problem by eliminating the evil of homelessness. Also, they must prove not only that their plan is desirable but that it offers definite and unassailable *advantages* over the present system. In so doing, they must convince the judge that their plan meets the need, and explain the advantages it represents. It will be the challenge of the negative team to counter the affirmative's advantages with much more convincing disadvantages. In other words, the negative team's goal is to convince the judge that the disadvantages outweigh the advantages.

These four stock issues are usually presented in

A POLICY DEBATER'S SCORECARD

If you are on the affirmative side, using logic, arguments, and evidence, you must be successful in proving all of the following stock issues.

Significance: that there is a significant problem with the present system.

Inherency: that the problem is central or inherent to the present system.

Solvency: that your plan will solve the problem.

Advantages: that your plan has major advantages over the present system.

Topicality: that you have responded to the problem exactly as it was presented and successfully answered all opposing arguments and evidence.

Bear in mind: If you fail in proving just one of the above stock issues, you will lose the debate.

If you are on the negative side, to win the debate you must prove the affirmative team wrong, inadequate, or insufficient in its efforts to prove at least one of these stock issues.

---

the first constructive speech in the debate, which is made by an affirmative team member. When this is done it is called a *prima facie* case. (*Prima facie* means "at first sight," or "before closer inspection.") *Prima facie* evidence is evidence that establishes a fact or raises a presumption of fact.

The fifth stock issue, *topicality*, has a direct bearing on the affirmative plan. To satisfy the requirements of this stock issue, the affirmative team must answer the problem exactly as worded in the resolution. It differs from the first four stock issues in that it is usually not mentioned in the first affirmative speech. Like all of the other stock issues, however, it represents another major challenge to negative team members, who must try to prove the affirmative wrong on all stock issues. If they succeed in doing this on only one stock issue, they will win the debate.

It is the obligation of the negative team to take wholly opposite points of view in each case and to argue them point for point by presenting evidence of their own. This provides the "clash" that is an essential element in every debate.[3]

The judge's decision is based on the logic of each side's arguments and on how well they are supported with evidence. In certain instances it may be possible to win an argument on logic alone, without evidence— in other words, by superior reasoning. But no argument can be won by a mere assertion. Saying that a particular argument is wrong or far-fetched or silly is pointless unless you can back up your assertion with convincing logic and evidence.

THREE

*P*REPARING FOR DEBATE

Once you know the resolution or proposition that will be debated and which team you will be on, affirmative or negative, your first step will be to begin the research. You and your team member will search through books, magazines, and other material that will help you find the evidence you need to present the strongest possible arguments to prove your case. A case consists of reasons, arguments, supporting facts, and other evidence presented in favor of or against a proposition. You will look for facts, studies, and arguments that support your side of the proposition. You will also look for the testimony of highly respected authorities. This includes evidence, reports, and statements by agencies, organizations, and individuals whose authority, knowledge, and experience are widely known and respected.

Through your research you will also become aware of some of the facts and arguments that the other side will probably use to prove their case. This is valuable information that you and your team member should include in your research notes. Later on you will find out just how valuable this information is.

WORKING WITH TEAM MEMBERS

As you continue your research, you and your team member should meet to compare notes on all the arguments you have discovered in favor of or against the proposition. This is how you analyze the proposition to find out the main issues involved. In your beginning research you will use the books, magazines, and other sources that your debating coach has reserved in the school library for this purpose. However, you should search out and be alert to other sources at your disposal in school and local libraries. In addition to other books, magazine articles, and official documents on the subject, this may include transcripts of national debates or speeches relating to the proposition.

As you and your team member study the information you have been gathering, certain strong points will emerge. These strong points—your most convincing evidence and arguments—will represent and support your stand on the main issues to be debated in the proposition.

THE MAIN ISSUES

In discovering the main issues, always keep in mind that it is not enough to concentrate only on your side of the issue or proposition. You must also be aware of, and take notes on, all the opposing arguments. This is the only way in which you can discover all of the main issues in a proposition. If you neglect to do this or are not as thorough in your analysis as you should be, one of the main issues that you and your team member have overlooked may turn out to be a major point on which the debate is lost.[1]

If you make the mistake of not studying your opponent's arguments, you may decide what you would like

ROTHCO
ORIGINAL

to prove. You may even discover the issues which you believe you can prove, based on the evidence you collect. You may feel confident that you have the advantage over your opponents. But you will not discover what you *must* prove in order to establish your case unless you know and understand what your opponents will be arguing.[2]

IMPORTANCE OF EVIDENCE

Remember, too, that opinion counts for nothing. You can have an opinion about anything under the sun, but no one will take it seriously unless you can show that it is based on some kind of evidence. The same goes for any argument you may use in a debate. It won't hold water unless it is strongly supported by evidence.

The British biologist Thomas Huxley once said that scientists develop "a valuable habit of believing nothing unless there is evidence for it; and they have a way of looking upon belief which is not based on evidence

The Quimby Debate Council Presents
An International Debate:

Was the Atomic Bombing of Hiroshima Justified?

Yes!
Sarah Watson '92
& Hajime Kawada,
Waseda University

No!
Dan Schwager '93
& Tomoyuki Uda,
Sophia University

Wed., Feb. 26 4 P.M.
Chase Lounge

Poster advertising a debate

not only as illogical but as immoral." The judge and audience observing a debate may not be scientists, but they will be no less willing to accept any argument that is not based on evidence. As you develop your skills as a debater, you will acquire the habit of neither offering nor accepting any statement as true unless it is based on evidence.

Here's a good example of using evidence to support an argument from a debate on "Who Belongs in the Loony Bin?" held June 6, 1990, in New York City. This was a *Firing Line* program, produced by the Southern Educational Communications Association, based in Columbia, South Carolina. Host William F. Buckley, Jr., took the opposing point of view against Kate Millet, an author who has questioned the whole concept of mental illness. Millet wrote *The Looney-Bin Trip*, in which she describes her psychiatric adventures when her family had her committed to a mental hospital where she was diagnosed as manic-depressive. In providing evidence about how easy it is to get another person committed to a mental hospital, especially a family member, she used her own personal experience, stating:

> *I see myself as one of millions of people who are treated this way. It's obscenely easy to get locked up. You have no rights. It was a very long time before I could get any legal help. Most people don't even know what their rights are. Immediately you are drugged; and to lose your liberty is a very serious thing, to lose your entire freedom of person. Everything that goes with being a responsible person and a citizen, at one stroke that is taken away. Think of all the good and cogent defenses that people have who commit crimes. The whole advocacy system, their rights are carefully protected.*
> *Here are people who have never broken*

any law and on somebody's word, if they even get a commitment hearing, it's going to last two minutes long, they will have a public defender who doesn't know them, they will very likely be drugged, the attorney who is assigned to them doesn't know them and will think they're crazy because the doctor said they're crazy, and the doctor is an expert.

YOU CAN'T FORCE BELIEF

Another point to keep in mind is that you can't force belief. According to one historical account, Christopher Columbus and his crew swore that the island of Cuba was the mainland of what came to be known as the Western Hemisphere, even though this had not been proven. Anyone on the ship who dared to contradict Columbus was told he would have his tongue slit.

We have long since learned that no one can be forced to believe in the truth of any argument unless it is based on fact, authority, or some other form of evidence. The same test applies to the written word as well as to the spoken word. The fact that a statement appears in print has nothing to do with its value as evidence unless it is based on fact or on the experience of a respected authority.[3]

THE STRENGTH OF THE EVIDENCE

You should remember not to overestimate the strength of your evidence. The evidence that you gather to prove your arguments will tend to fall into three categories. Some may offer possible proof, some probable proof, and some actual proof. No matter how impressive it may seem to you, all of the evidence you present taken together, in most cases will seldom prove more than a high degree of probability.[4] If it is strong enough, you have a good chance of winning the debate.

Once you and your partner have agreed on the main issues you will be arguing, you will select the best evidence to support your arguments. Taking research notes in a random manner will waste time and may result in confusion. Your research should be well organized, and so should your system of taking notes.

TAKING NOTES

One method of taking notes is to use either separate sheets of paper or four-by-six-inch note cards, writing only on one side. The notes on each sheet or card should refer to only one topic, either a main point or a subordinate point. Put the title of the topic at the top of the sheet or card.

Be selective in your notes. Note only those words that clearly and convincingly support your arguments. Quote directly from the source you are using, and indicate this by putting quotation marks around the words quoted. Make sure your reference to the source is complete. For instance, in the case of books and magazine articles it should include the name of the author, the title of the book or magazine article plus the name of the magazine, and the date of publication. Although only a small portion of the evidence you collect will be used during the debate, you need this pool of information to draw from when you respond to any challenges, arguments, and refutations.

SELECTING EVIDENCE

Once your initial research has been completed, you and your partner will meet to discuss the results and compare notes with each other and your debate coach. If you have all the evidence and arguments you need, the research could end there. If you all agree that it's not complete enough, then you will need to spend more time gathering evidence so that you can build a stronger case.

All of the information you gather will be used to serve your needs in the two major phases of a debate—the opening statement and the rebuttal—no matter what type of debate it happens to be. The opening statement, or constructive speech, is made by the team member who speaks first for both the affirmative and negative sides. The strongest arguments must be presented within the time limit allowed. In the standard debate format this is followed by constructive speeches by the second team member on each side. All the arguments or challenges made by the opposing team member who spoke first should be answered in this speech. It should also strongly reinforce the team's major arguments.

The constructive speeches are followed by rebuttal speeches. This is your last opportunity to convince the judge that reason, logic, and the best evidence are on your side. Usually a shorter time is allowed for rebuttals than for constructive speeches. Following is the format used in standard debating:[5]

STANDARD DEBATING FORMAT

First constructive speech by affirmative team	10 minutes
First constructive speech by negative team	10 minutes
Second constructive speech by affirmative team	10 minutes
Second constructive speech by negative team	10 minutes
First rebuttal by negative team	5 minutes
First rebuttal by affirmative team	5 minutes
Second rebuttal by negative team	5 minutes
Second rebuttal by affirmative team	5 minutes

No matter what type of debate you are involved in, generally speaking there will be three basic conditions: (1) both sides must have an equal number of speakers; (2) both sides must have an equal amount of time; and (3) the affirmative side must speak first and last.[6]

DON'T GET SIDETRACKED

Because of the time factors involved, and to increase your team's chances of winning the debate, you must be careful to keep to the main issues and not get sidetracked into less convincing facts and arguments. This caution should be taken in both constructive speech and rebuttal. Never lose sight of your objective. You know that whatever arguments your side makes will be opposed. You must be prepared to meet them head-on with even more convincing counter-arguments in your rebuttal.[7]

A good example of finding the main issues can be found in a letter President Abraham Lincoln wrote to Major General George B. McClellan during the Civil War. Before he wrote the letter, Lincoln lined up all that could be said in favor of McClellan's plan against all that could be said in favor of his own plan. Here is the letter:

Executive Mansion   *February 3, 1862*
Washington, D.C.

Major General McClellan.
My dear sir:—You and I have distinct and different plans for a movement of the Army of the Potomac—yours to be down the Chesapeake, up the Rappahannock to Urbana, and across land to the terminus of the railroad on the York River; mine to move directly to a point on the railroad southwest of Manassas.
If you will give me satisfactory answers to

the following questions, I shall gladly yield my plan to yours.

First. Does not your plan involve a greatly larger expenditure of time and money than mine?

Second. Wherein is a victory more certain by your plan than mine?

Third. Wherein is a victory more valuable by your plan than mine?

Fourth. In fact, would it not be less valuable in this, that it would break no great line of the enemy's communications, while mine would?

Fifth. In case of disaster, would not a retreat be more difficult by your plan than mine?

Yours truly,
Abraham Lincoln

One of the most respected authorities on the art and science of debating, William Trufant Foster, described finding the main issues in this way: "There is a main issue in all the affairs of life. Success depends on directing effort toward that issue. Without the ability to analyze a given situation and discover the particular difficulty to overcome, i.e., the main issue, a man may waste his energy in blind endeavor, like a fly trying to escape through a window."

"HITTING THE NAIL ON THE HEAD"

According to Foster, the primary objective in discovering the main issues is to do so without getting sidetracked on unimportant or subordinate issues. He declared: "A thousand hard blows around a nail will not move it. One hard blow on the head will drive it in. The method of (finding) the main issue may be described as 'hitting the nail on the head.' "

Lincoln's letter to McClellan is an example of a

good beginning in discovering the main issues. He fully acknowledged opposing views but countered with more convincing arguments that supported his views. Before he reached that point, however, we can assume that he spent a lot of time studying, thinking about, and discussing the problem.

PREPARING FOR A DEBATE

1. Through research, find the arguments and evidence you need in books, magazines, reports, studies, and other authoritative sources.
2. Use separate note cards or sheets of paper for each main issue, argument, or topic.
3. Also make notes on the opposition's most likely arguments and have the counter-arguments and evidence you need to refute them.
4. Compare research notes with your partner. Work closely together in completing the research your team needs to build a convincing case.
5. As the final preparatory step, decide which are the main issues and select the best evidence to support your arguments in your constructive speech and to refute your opponents in your rebuttal speech.

FOUR

METHODS OF ARGUMENT

Whatever the proposition you will be debating, you will use certain techniques of *logic* and *argumentation*— some consciously, some unconsciously. First, let's review the differences between logic and argumentation. According to one authority, the main purpose of logic is to make it possible for individuals and groups to distinguish between good and bad reasoning.[1]

In argumentation the main purpose is to convince and persuade people and urge them to action. Logic, then, is concerned only with reason. Argumentation is concerned not only with logical or convincing arguments but with influencing belief or action through the appeal to emotion. It is through logic and argumentation that each team attempts to convince and persuade the judge that its arguments in favor or against the proposition are stronger and therefore more convincing.

SOME BASIC METHODS OF REASONING

Two common methods of reasoning used in debate are *inductive* reasoning and *deductive* reasoning. In inductive reasoning you start with specific facts or exam-

ples and thereby reach a generalization or conclusion. Here's an example of inductive reasoning:

> There are nine known planets in the solar system: Mercury, Venus, Earth, Mars, Jupiter, Saturn, Uranus, Neptune, and Pluto. Each of these planets orbits around the sun. Therefore, you can say as a generalization or conclusion that all the known planets in the solar system orbit around the sun.

Deductive reasoning works in the opposite way, moving from the general to the specific. Here's an example:

> Any person who is legally insane is considered incompetent to make a binding legal agree-

*ment. Joan Bill is legally insane. Therefore,
Joan Bill is incompetent to make a binding legal
agreement.*

Both of these examples are extremely simple, but they
illustrate the basic structures of these types of reasoning. Here are examples of inductive and deductive
reasoning from a *Firing Line* debate March 3, 1991 on
the following resolution: "Resolved: Drug Prohibition
Has Failed." One of the affirmative team members,
Richard Dennis, a commodity trader, president of *New
Perspectives Quarterly*, and member of the Chicago
Council on Foreign Relations, used inductive reasoning in arguing that the government had failed to play an
effective moral role in the war against the illegal use of
drugs. He declared:

> *I suspect at some point tonight the other side
> will be tired of statistics they can't refute, and
> we will hear that the war on drugs is a moral
> issue. Now unfortunately the first principle of a
> just war is that you do more good—that you
> don't cause more harm than the good you aim
> to achieve. And that's a moral question, and it
> seems to me the war on drugs fails that test
> miserably. Of course, we can't be fooled. The
> war on drugs is a moral issue, and it seems to
> me that that's exactly why the government
> shouldn't be involved.*
>   *The last time I checked, the government
> was greedily collecting taxes from alcohol
> sales, was lavishly subsidizing tobacco, and
> had replaced the mob in the numbers game.
> They call it the state lottery. Actually, the gov-
> ernment's attitude on the war on drugs poisons
> the moral atmosphere on a daily basis. We're
> egged on to hate the sinner instead of the sin*

by egregious statements about beheading dealers and executing users, and actually I think we heard a few more egregious statements here tonight.

I think we should remember that salvation— although we have experts on the other side who are more able to talk about salvation than I—is an individual exercise, not a collective one. The idea of government as moralist is both tragic and comic.

One of the opposing team members, Lois Herrington, a lawyer who served as chairman of the White House Conference for a Drug Free America during the Reagan Administration, used deductive reasoning in attempts to disprove that there had ever been a true prohibition against drugs. She began her argument by stating:

The proposition tonight assumes that we have had drug prohibition, and we have not.

In the '60s and '70s we stopped building prisons while serious crime rose 400 percent. We sent out a message that drugs were okay, and our youth stood in line. We glamourized drugs in our words, in our music, and lives were lost. The values of a society are measured by the penalty imposed when these values are violated. By that standard, Americans should be judged derelict in their duty to their fellow citizens and even to posterity.

For every 100 violent crimes in America two criminals go to prison. The median time served by drug traffickers in state prisons is 14 months. Most Americans believe drug dealers are getting out of prison old and poor. The fact is, most aren't going. And the ones that do are getting out young and rich. Crime pays. Do we then raise the flag of surrender as some here tonight would do, condemning the many who come after us to lifelong slavery?

In the past few years we have seen a beginning: education, prevention, treatment, tougher laws, and changes in self-destructive attitudes have begun to work. Drug use is down. And Americans all across the country are beginning to say, "Not in my home, not in my school, not in my neighborhood, not in my state, and not in my nation." Prohibition can succeed if it's meaningful. Almost every recovering addict and treatment-provider will tell you, "Make it difficult to use. Very difficult to use. Because if you don't, the seductiveness of the high will win."

THE WEIGHT OF THE EVIDENCE

You will probably use many methods of reasoning in presenting your case for or against a proposition. Other methods are explored in the chapters that follow on affirmative and negative strategies. In argumentation, which is what debating is all about, the main concern is to show the likelihood that a given proposition is true or false, proved or disproved through logic, reasoning, evidence, and all the other elements of argumentation.[2]

The limits of time to research and debate a proposition, as well as the complexity of the proposition itself, in almost every case will make it impossible to prove that it is absolutely true or false under all circumstances.

Even though you may show great skill in using inductive and deductive reasoning and other methods to prove your arguments, you cannot expect to prove your arguments conclusively. Your goal must be to show that the weight of the evidence, in other words, the strongest evidence and arguments, is on your side.[3]

Your opponents will also be using inductive and deductive reasoning and other methods to prove their case. But if there are flaws in their arguments you should be alert to point them out in your rebuttal. This is something the judge will expect you to do, otherwise you will lose points and may lose the debate. Here's an example of how Lincoln exposed a major flaw in Douglas's reasoning:

> *The states must, without the interference of the General Government, do all those things that pertain exclusively to themselves—that are local in nature, that have no connection with the General Government.*
>
> *After Judge Douglas has established this proposition which nobody disputes or ever has disputed, he proceeds to assume, without proving it, that slavery is one of those little, unimportant, trivial matters, which are of just about as much consequence as the question would be to me whether my neighbor should raise horned cattle or plant tobacco; that there is no moral question about it, but that it is altogether a matter of dollars and cents.*
>
> *That when a new territory is opened for settlement, the first man who goes into it may plant there a thing which, like the Canada thistle, or some other pests of the soil, cannot be dug out by the millions of men who will come thereafter; that it is one of those little things that is so trivial in its nature that it has no effect upon anybody save the few men who first plant upon the soil.*
>
> *That it is not a thing which in any way affects*

the family of communities composing those states, nor in any way endangers the General Government. Judge Douglas ignores altogether the very well-known fact that we have never had a serious menace to our political existence, except it sprang from this thing, which he chooses to regard as only upon a par with onions and potatoes.

CHALLENGES TO YOUR ARGUMENTS

Your opponents, in their efforts to prove their case and thereby disprove yours, will highlight all the important exceptions to whatever arguments you make and whatever conclusions you offer as evidence. These are the challenges that create excitement in a debate. They also put you on the defensive and make you work harder to prove your case.

One way in which to deflate some of the threatening evidence presented by your opponents is to admit all that you can safely admit, but no more.[4] But be cautious. Admitting a point or argument that dangerously weakens your case can make the difference between winning or losing a debate. For this reason, in preparing for a debate you must know and understand all the possible opposing arguments to your stand on the proposition and be well prepared to answer them.

When a minor point is made, one that you are certain cannot in any way damage your case, then it is safe to admit it. In doing this you take some of the bite out of your opponents' charges. However, you must be prepared to counter with a strong argument.

This will make the minor point appear even less significant, and you will thereby strengthen your case. When charges are made that you cannot safely admit, it is even more important to counter with the strongest possible arguments that support your position.

FIVE

MAKING YOUR DELIVERY EFFECTIVE

The preferred method of delivery in debating and other forms of public speaking is to speak extemporaneously, that is, without reading from a prepared statement. However, this is an art that requires several years and wide experience for most people to master. As a beginning debater you should concentrate on another alternative: skillful speaking from carefully organized notes. This, too, is an art, if it is to be done well.

One method you may want to use in learning this art is to write out your opening statement, or constructive speech, in its entirety, making sure you have covered all the main points.[1] Then condense this material down to an outline, using complete sentences for the main points and partial sentences or phrases for the evidence that supports them.

Then practice speaking from your outline, filling in with appropriate words where complete sentences are needed. Take care that your speech has continuity, without any long pauses in delivery. The more you practice, the less likely there will be any long, noticeable pauses. Eventually it will begin to sound fluent and polished, just the way you want it to sound when you make your constructive speech during the debate.

*Republican Vice Presidential candidate Dan Quayle
(l) sparred with the Democratic candidate Al Gore (r)
as independent-party candidate James Stockdale
looked on during the 1992 Vice Presidential debates.*

A SAMPLE OUTLINE

The following resolution was once suggested by the
National Forensic League as a possible topic to be
used by high school debaters.

*Resolved: That the Federal Government Should
Significantly Increase Social Services to Homeless Individuals in the United States.*

Now, suppose you were chosen by your debate coach to make the first affirmative constructive speech in an upcoming debate on this resolution. After you have done the research, here's a sample outline on which you might base your constructive speech:

  I. *The number of men, women, and children in the United States now suffering the ravages of homelessness is a national disgrace.*
     A. *Summary of most recent government statistics*
     B. *Reports from the U.S. Department of Health and Human Services*
     C. *Quotes from editorials published in* The New York Times *and other highly respected print media*
 II. *Existing federal programs fall far short of meeting the physical and psychological needs of the homeless.*
     A. *Examples from studies of the homeless in the state capital and other major cities in your state*
     B. *Examples of burdens this situation places on nongovernment agencies and organizations trying to meet the most essential needs*
III. *The federal government has a moral obligation to help the homeless.*
     A. *Summarize guarantees found in the U.S. Constitution, the Bill of Rights, and other amendments to the Constitution*
     B. *Federal programs and recent legislation in which the federal government has demonstrated its moral awareness and responsibilities in meeting other social problems*
 IV. *Summing Up: The major arguments and ev-*

idence that show clearly and poignantly the plight of the homeless and the need for swift and substantial government action.

IMPROVING YOUR VOICE

When you are debating, a great deal of the judge's and audience's attention will be focused on your voice. Be sure of the pronounciation of words and use a variety of tones so your voice won't sound monotonous. Also, be sure to emphasize the main points of your arguments, using good vocal techniques. These and other qualities you bring to your presentation can help or hinder the persuasiveness of your arguments.[2] Spending enough time rehearsing your constructive speech will help. So will the use of a tape recorder so you can hear exactly how you sound.

Students who sing in a chorus or church choir have one advantage in that they have learned how to control their breathing and how to make pleasant-sounding tones. This can enhance their speaking voice and help them make long statements without pausing for breath. Even if you are not a singer, you can develop an attractive speaking voice by using certain vocal exercises and techniques recommended for speakers.

For example, practice expelling the air from your lungs in short, sharp gasps. As you do this, place your hand on your abdomen so you can feel the tightening or inward contraction of your stomach muscles as air is expelled from your lungs. Then try using sounds as air is expelled. Say "hep! hep! hep!" or "bah, bay, bee, bi, bo, boo," or some other combination of sounds.

ANOTHER BREATHING EXERCISE

Another exercise to improve control over breathing is to fill your lungs with air and then exhale as slowly as possible. Time yourself to see how long you can keep exhaling without stopping. Keep in mind that the object is not to get as much air as you can into your lungs but how slowly you can let the air out.

Then try vocalizing again. As you slowly let the air out of your lungs, utter a long, continuous hum. Then try an "oo" sound and other vowel sounds. Don't let the sound become "breathy." Keep the tone clear. One way to make sure the air is being let out of your lungs as slowly as possible is to hold a lighted candle close to your mouth. The flame should flicker but not go out.

IMPROVING TONE QUALITY

Using the words in the list below, intone each word quietly at first and then louder and louder. Try to give the tone a ringing quality by letting the word vibrate in your throat. Avoid breathiness by not using too much air. As you intone the words, put your fingertips on your nose and cheekbones to see if you can feel a vibration. The stronger the vibration the better the tone.

one	home	drone	alone	phone
rain	plain	nine	lean	spoon
ring	nine	gong	moon	fine

MAKING YOUR WORDS DISTINCT

Another good exercise for improving voice quality as well as pronunciation is to read aloud a favorite passage from prose or poetry, or a lyric from a favorite song. Do this slowly at first, making sure all of the words are pronounced correctly, and then faster until you've reached a normal rate of speaking.

You can improve the clarity of your speaking voice by paying special attention to the distinctness of the words. As clearly and rapidly as you can, practice saying tongue-twisters such as the following:

She sells sea shells by the sea shore.
National Shropshire Sheep Association.
Are you copper-bottoming them, my man?
No, I'm aluminuming 'em, mum.
He sawed six long, slim, sleek, slender sap-
lings.
Dick twirled the stick athwart the path.
Rubber baby-buggy bumpers.
Sarah, Sarah, sitting in a shoe shine shop.

VOWELS AND CONSONANTS

Improving the distinctness of your speech through careful enunciation of vowels and consonants will lend persuasiveness to your constructive speech and rebuttal. As one debating expert cautioned: "Many people swallow their vowels and ignore their consonants. Especially flagrant is this fault at the end of sentences, which as a rule should deserve the greatest emphasis. Earnest, sustained practice in enunciation is necessary. It may be exaggerated in practice with no danger of exaggeration in public."[3] All of the words you speak in a debate are important. It is your responsibility to make sure they are heard and given the emphasis they deserve.

WHEN YOU GET UP TO SPEAK

You probably won't be able to avoid a certain amount of nervousness when you get up to speak. This is natural, and to a certain degree it is good for you because it tends to heighten your awareness and your desire to perform well. However, do whatever you can to control your nervousness and not let it detract from your delivery. How you stand and act during your delivery is important.

Try to look ready and relaxed. Avoid any eccentricities that will be distracting, such as slouching, long pauses, speaking too slowly or too quickly. Stand erect, speak straightforwardly, and be as composed as you can.

Avoid flamboyant gestures to emphasize major points. As a general rule, deliberate gestures are not necessary in debating. Whatever gestures come as you speak, such as raising your arms, pointing a finger, making a fist, making a sweeping motion with your hand, for example, should come naturally. Do not make conscious gestures.

If you are well prepared and interested in your subject, there will be a certain amount of body movement and gesturing, but it will never be exaggerated, and will therefore not distract from your delivery.

Speak as naturally as possible, with no pretense, no staginess that will turn off the judge and audience. If you tend to overdo certain gestures, even though they may come naturally, your coach will point this out to you.

READING QUOTATIONS

Rather than commit all of the evidence to memory or depend on an outline and notes, occasionally you may want to read a quotation directly from the source, such as a book, magazine, or government report. This can be very effective. However, you must practice reading the quotation aloud so you can make your point as effectively as possible.[4]

You don't want to stumble in the reading, giving the judge and audience the impression you aren't familiar with the material. Also, continue to make eye contact with the judge while reading, never taking your eyes off him or her for more than a second or two.

Note the words you want to emphasize and have the section you want to read well marked so you can find it quickly. Time is of the essence, strictly limited in both constructive speech and rebuttal. Reading the exact words from one of your most important sources of evidence will tend to increase its credibility. However, don't do this so often that it becomes distracting and monotonous.

PRACTICING YOUR DELIVERY

Once you have written your opening statement in full and then condensed it into an outline, the next step is to practice your delivery. This will be difficult to do smoothly until you have practiced many times. As you go through this step in preparation, the important thing is not to get discouraged. Even though there may be occasional pauses at first, as you put your thoughts in order, remembering all the details you want to include and putting them into interesting sentences, keep going over the material until your delivery is as smooth as you can make it.

Time yourself to see how many of the main points you can include in your constructive speech in the time allowed for it. When you begin to feel confident about your delivery, practice in front of a friend or family member and ask them to be critical. This will help you improve your delivery and eliminate any eccentricities or gestures that are inappropriate or distracting.

Ask the person listening to you the kinds of questions that will be helpful, such as: Is the language clear? Is the argument convincing? Am I emphasizing the right words? Make your style of delivery conversational. Speak as if you were talking to a small group of friends or classmates.[5] Don't be stiff and "oratorical."

Make your transitions as smooth as possible as you move from point to point. There are many ways in which you can do this. For example, change the rate of delivery, the tone, the volume, or your position as you address the judge and audience. Other methods include changing the emphasis, using a gesture that comes naturally, and skillfully using pauses.

HOW TO USE EMPHASIS

You'll know which are the strongest points in your argument, but to highlight their importance you must give them sufficient emphasis. The judge and audience won't be sifting through your arguments to find out which are the strongest. You will have to indicate this and make those arguments memorable.

One recommended technique is to utter the words in a major argument with concentrated deliberation. Stop abruptly and pause in the right places. Use a natural gesture to attract attention. Lower your tone and slow the rate of delivery, or increase the volume and the pace. Anything you can do to increase the attention to your main points will help you give them the emphasis they deserve.

A PERSUASIVE AND CONVINCING DELIVERY

Through good delivery techniques, do whatever you can to make your constructive speech and your rebuttal persuasive and convincing. One way to do this is to put your full concentration on what you are saying. The message—what you say and how you say it—should be your chief concern. For this reason a simple, direct approach is the best technique. Don't beat around the bush. Come right to the point and stay with it throughout your delivery.

In your rebuttal you can show you are fair-minded by admitting some points that are safe to admit. Give your opponents their due, as long as your arguments are not damaged. Never avoid an important issue raised by your opponents or you will lose points.[6] Also, fairness in itself can be persuasive because it demonstrates to the judge that you understand both sides of the question. Try to maintain good self-control and don't let your emotions get the upper hand.

This is particularly important in your rebuttal speech in which you are responding directly to your opponents. Answer their arguments clearly and firmly, and restate your own arguments as strongly and emphatically as possible.

If you can think of a humorous situation, story, or analogy that exposes a weakness in your opponents' arguments, you may want to consider injecting some humor into your presentation. This can be effective as long as the humor is appropriate. However, the humor should be brief and not take precious time away from the main thrust of your arguments.

When you are using humor to drive home a point or to expose your opponents' errors in reasoning, make sure the judge and audience are laughing with you and not at you. Nothing is more wasted or pointless than humor that has nothing to do with the arguments involved in debating a proposition.[7]

A PERSUASIVE SPEAKER

In learning how to be a persuasive speaker you will realize that people are willing to be led if they are convinced your arguments are reasonable. But you can't force them to think as you do, or to accept your opinions and arguments. You must persuade them.[8] In doing this you must also appeal to their emotions.

But persuasion will not be possible unless you speak with conviction and convince the judge that your side has the stronger arguments. Use all the recommended speaking techniques you can master in reaching this objective. However, remember that conviction is a matter of reason, and reason is based on logic. Your arguments must be logical and your evidence must be convincing.

SIX

*T*AKING THE AFFIRMATIVE SIDE

To be successful in affirmative debating, you must accomplish three objectives:

1. You must be able to state clearly what must be done to establish the proof of a proposition.
2. You must accomplish this objective by means of convincing arguments.
3. Through reason *and* emotion your arguments must be so convincing that you will persuade the judge that you have proved the proposition.

YOUR OPENING STATEMENT

To accomplish these objectives you must concentrate on the main issues. These are the points on which the proofs of the proposition depend. In the first part of your constructive speech, present the main issues clearly. Then state how you intend to prove that these issues exist and that they support the affirmative's stand on the proposition.[1]

In other words, you are saying to the judge, "If I can

prove these points, I can prove the proposition." You then proceed to argue your case, making it clear that you are doing what you said you would do to prove the proposition. At the close of your constructive speech, summarize what you have done to prove your case and state that you believe you have done so convincingly.[2]

Here's an excerpt from a constructive speech made by Glenn Loury, professor of political economy at Boston University, who, at the time, was writing a book on the problem of racial inequality in America. He was speaking as a member of the affirmative team in a debate held August 28, 1991 and telecast by the Public Broadcasting System on the following resolution:

Resolved: Freedom of Thought Is in Danger on American Campuses.

Professor Loury declared:

A professor of economics, lecturing with inputs on the axes, says "man-hours," and a committee of women visits him after the class and instructs him that, "No, man-hours is not acceptable language to quantify the amount of labor that's being used."

In a class about civics, the movie It's a Wonderful Life *is used to illustrate the principles being taught. The film has to be withdrawn because a committee of students visits the professor and instructs him that the black woman in the movie is portrayed in a degrading way.*

Students are reprimanded or criticized publicly by a university administrator because they organize a theme party around the 1950s and they're told that, well, the 1950s was a time of racism and such a party by students is offensive to others.

A professor of law refers to one of his colleagues as, "Well, he may look black, but he thinks white."

These examples could be multiplied. The point here is not of course that the forces of restriction of thought and expression are carrying people off to dungeons somewhere. The point is that the social pressures and the consequences of engaging in certain kinds of discourse are very severe.

Things that can't be talked about on campus today:

Are homosexual acts immoral?

Can we talk about the extent of differences, overt differences, in academic performance between racial groups?

Can we discuss whether or not certain affirmative action practices are effective policy for the university?

In other words, there are real restrictions on the scope of debate that can take place.

CLAIMING MORE THAN YOU CAN PROVE

In the conclusion to your constructive speech be careful not to claim more than you believe you have proved. If you claim more than you have actually proved, the judge will probably react in one of two ways. He or she will think you are trying to deceive the judge in regard to the strength of your evidence, or that you have deceived yourself.[3] If this happens, your other arguments and evidence may be viewed with suspicion.

Don't exaggerate, don't argue that you have proved the proposition beyond the shadow of a doubt. End with a strong conclusion, but don't assume that your evidence is beyond challenge. If the proposition wasn't subject to controversy or argument, why would you be debating it?

A good example of what you might expect if you claim more than you can prove can be seen in the following response by Professor Ronald Walters, chairman of the political science department at Howard University and former president of the African Heritage Studies Association. His response was made as a member of the negative team in the aforementioned debate. He denied that freedom of thought on American campuses was in danger, contending that the affirmative team had claimed more than it could prove.

> I think sometimes, given this question of the extended degree to which we want freedom, that we forget about responsibility, and we forget about the fact that in our Constitution there is something in the preamble which talks about ensuring domestic tranquility. I think that's still a very laudable aim, not only in society, but also on the university campus. I actually was reading another document when I picked that up, because I had almost forgotten it. It was the Kerner Commission report on the causes and prevention of violence.
>
> What they sought to do in 1968 in trying to explain how this country burst aflame in violence and how it was so important to develop a new regime of civility was to go back to this phrase in the Constitution, and I think it's very important. Because on our campuses today many minorities are suffering something which has been called "ethnoviolence." As a matter of fact, from 800,000 to a million students are suffering this, according to one reputable organization, and something should be done about it.

THE REBUTTAL SPEECH

In your rebuttal speech your research and understanding of both sides of the issue you are debating will provide you with the ammunition you need. So will careful attention to the arguments presented by your opponents.[4] The time to prepare your rebuttal speech will be limited. In whatever time is allowed, be ready to sift through your notes and select whatever new evidence and arguments you need to answer challenges made by the opposition and to reinforce your stand on the proposition.

As you listen to your opponents' constructive speeches you should be making notes on your *flowsheet,* jotting down key words or phrases that will direct you to the evidence you need. These are the facts and statements from authoritative sources that will give you the ammunition you need to deny or minimize your opponents' arguments while at the same time strengthening your own.

The rebuttal speech is an essential part of any debate. It gives both sides the opportunity to expand and reinforce their arguments. If a debate consisted only of constructive speeches by both sides it would be the beginning but not the completion of what a debate is intended to be: a spirited clash of opinions. The affirmative side essentially presents a constructive case in favor of the proposition. That intention and goal must be maintained in the rebuttal speech.

However, the rebuttal speech is also destructive in the sense that its purpose is to destroy or deny the arguments made by the negative side. As one debating authority expressed it: "Those who are to be convinced of the truth of a proposition wish to know not only why the arguments in favor are sound but also why the opposing arguments are unsound."[5]

There are two basic ways in which you can attack your opponents' arguments. One deals with the facts

TIPS FOR REBUTTALS

- Preparation for an effective rebuttal speech must include research in which the major and minor arguments on both sides of the issue are fully understood and noted.
- When opposing team members are speaking, be quick to jot down key words and phrases that will direct you to arguments and evidence in your notes that you'll want to use in your rebuttal speech.
- Remember that the time to prepare your rebuttal speech will be limited. You must be prepared to act quickly in sifting through your notes to select the strongest arguments and evidence.
- Be sure to respond to all of your opponents' arguments with counterarguments and evidence of your own. Restate the major arguments you believe will convince the judge that the preponderance of logic, reason, and evidence is on your side.
- Keep in mind that the purpose of an affirmative team member's rebuttal is to destroy or deny the arguments of the negative side, pointing out errors in reasoning and other flaws while at the same time presenting your strongest case in favor of the proposition.

or evidence presented, the other with the soundness of their reasoning. As to facts presented by your opponents, you can challenge the value and importance of those facts or show with evidence of your own that the facts supporting your case are stronger. As to the soundness of your opponents' reasoning, there are several types of unsound reasoning you can attack in your rebuttal speech. One is mistaking the cause for the effect.

A good example of this can be found in the debate between O'Connell of Ireland and Macaulay of England in Britain's House of Lords in 1833. O'Connell argued that the Act of Union, uniting Ireland with Great Britain, should be repealed—in other words, that Ireland should be allowed to govern its own country. The main issue he raised in favor of this argument concerned the disastrous conditions then existing in Ireland, for which he blamed the Union. In his rebuttal speech Macaulay gave the following answer:

> *Ireland has undoubtedly just causes of complaint. We heard those causes recapitulated last night by the honorable and learned member, who tells us that he represents not Dublin alone, but Ireland, and that he stands between his country and civil war.*
>
> *I do not deny that most of the grievances which he recounted exist, that they are serious, and that they ought to be remedied as far as it is in the power of legislation to remedy them. What I do deny is that they were caused by the Union, and that the Repeal of the Union would remove them. I listened attentively while the honorable and learned gentleman went through that long and melancholy list, and I am confident that he did not mention a single evil which was not a subject of bitter complaint while Ireland had a domestic parliament.*
>
> *Is it fair, is it reasonable in the honorable gentleman to impute to the Union evils which, as he knows better than any other in the house, existed long before the Union?* Post hoc: ergo, propter hoc [*after this, therefore on account of*

*it] is not always sound reasoning. But ante hoc:
ergo, non propter hoc [before this, therefore not
on account of it] is unanswerable.*

*The old rustic who told Sir Thomas More
that Tenterden Steeple was the cause of Goodwin Sands reasoned much better than the honorable and learned gentleman. For it was not till
after Tenterden Steeple was built that the fright-
ful wrecks on the Goodwin Sands were heard
of. But the honorable and learned gentleman
would make Goodwin Sands the cause of Tenterden Steeple.*

*Some of the Irish grievances which he as-
cribes to the Union are not only older than the
Union, but are not peculiarly Irish. They are
common to England, Scotland, and Ireland;
and it was in order to get rid of them that we, for
the common benefit of England, Ireland, and
Scotland, passed the Reform Bill last year.*

A more contemporary example of how errors in reasoning can be attacked is found in the following rebuttal by
Leon Botstein, president of Bard College, arguing in
the debate mentioned earlier about freedom of thought
on American campuses. President Botstein declared
that the issue was not freedom of thought but fear and
lack of courage to speak out against trends, move-
ments, ideas, attitudes, regulations, or practices. He
declared:

*There has never been a high degree of freedom
of thought in the university in the way that critics
now accuse us of not having. People didn't
speak out against dominant trends twenty or
thirty years ago, against fascism in the '30s or
during the McCarthy era in the '50s. We don't
have high marks for freedom of thought. There*

is probably more freedom of thought now than there was thirty or forty years ago. So we're also suffering from false nostalgia.

People are remembering once upon a time we had standards and a great education. Well, every alumni gathering I come to disproves this. I prefer that they don't believe they've read Aristotle than the notion they've read it and have so little to show for it.

The other issue, of course, is that the university is being held accountable for an intolerance in society which both sides are guilty of. We don't want to listen to the other person. We don't believe that discourse, discussion, is actually going to change someone's mind. And therefore we only want to be satisfied by symbolic labels.

We don't have the language or the educational quality that is able actually to conduct dissent. The Supreme Court doesn't want dissent; no one wants dissent. And we suffer that problem on our students and do not know how to teach tolerance and dissent.

SEVEN

HOW THE NEGATIVE ATTACKS

You must be thoroughly prepared in order to make a successful attack against the affirmative team's arguments. This means you must not only present effective arguments against the proposition but also know the strengths and weaknesses of the affirmative's side.

The same three steps that the affirmative side should take in preparing arguments in favor of the proposition should also be taken by the negative side.

1. You must be able to set forth clearly and concisely what must be done to overthrow the proposition.
2. You must do this by using convincing arguments and evidence.
3. You must be persuasive enough in your reasoning and in your emotional appeal to convince the judge that you have won the debate.

You must use the time allowed for your opening statement to present the main issues raised by the proposition. At the same time you should tell the judge why you disagree with the affirmative side and how you intend to prove your case. The key to your team's success is preparation. Know all the probable and possible arguments the affirmative side may use and be prepared to counter with effective arguments of your own. If you are better prepared than the affirmative side, this could give you enough of an advantage to win the debate.

THE PROBABLE ARGUMENTS

It's extremely important to study your opponents' probable arguments. You can do this successfully only by analyzing the proposition thoroughly enough to understand the main arguments on both sides of the question. Be careful not to sidestep or ignore important points in the argument, even though they do not help to prove your case.[1] Senator Douglas made this mistake in his debates with Abraham Lincoln on the slavery issue. Here's an example of how Lincoln exposed Douglas:

> *It is precisely upon that part of the history of the country that one important omission is made by Judge Douglas. He selects parts of the history of the United States upon the subject of slavery and treats it as the whole, omitting from his historical sketch the legislation of Congress in regard to the admission of Missouri, by which the Missouri Compromise was established and slavery excluded from a country [the Missouri Territory] half as large as the present United States.*

Commentary: Here Lincoln accuses Douglas of ignoring the significance of the Missouri Compromise, an act of Congress in which the practice of slavery was forbidden in that territory. There is the added implication here that members of Congress, who are elected by the people, are duty bound to reflect the will of the people in their districts on whatever question they vote on. Therefore, this antislavery measure reflects the will of the people on this crucial question.

Lincoln continued:

All this is left out of his history. And hence I ask how extraordinary a thing it is that a man who has occupied a position upon the floor of the Senate of the United States, who is now in his third term, and who looks to see the government of this whole country fall into his hands, pretending to give a truthful and accurate history of the slavery question in this country, should so entirely ignore the whole portion of that history—the most important of all.

Commentary: Lincoln again drives his point home, holding Douglas up to ridicule for pretending to speak on the entire slavery issue but ignoring this essential part of its history.

Lincoln continued:

Is it not a most extraordinary spectacle that a man should stand up and ask for any confidence in his statements, who sets out as he does with portions of history, calling upon the people to believe that it is a true and fair representation, when the leading part and controlling feature of the whole history is carefully suppressed?

Commentary: This is Lincoln's way of saying that Douglas is being dishonest in his discussion of the slavery issue and therefore his judgment (and his arguments) should not be trusted. This is a good example of emphasizing an important point or argument through repetition.

SELECTING THE STRONGEST EVIDENCE

In your research you will discover a great deal of usable evidence to support your side of the proposition. It is good to find as much evidence as you can to make your arguments as strong as possible, but it can also be a problem unless you use it wisely. Using the first evidence that comes to hand is a poor approach and may weaken your argument.[2] Keep collecting evidence within the time allowed for research, but once it has been collected there are decisions to be made.

You must select only the strongest evidence that supports your case and put the other evidence aside. One reason to hold onto it is that you might want to refer to some of it in your rebuttal if your opponents make reference to it in their constructive speeches.

Your approach in gathering evidence can be summed up in the words of one debating expert who said a debater should "read, read, read" and "think, think, think. And all the time he should be judiciously selecting, weighing, comparing, and rejecting." He also cautioned, "Let all the good pieces of evidence struggle for places in the argument: the law of selection must be the survival of the fittest."

Whatever evidence you decide to use, be careful not to overestimate its strength. No matter how strong your evidence may be, in all likelihood it will be conclusive only insofar as it demonstrates strong probability. For this reason, be careful not to claim more than the evidence justifies. If you exaggerate its worth you will weaken your argument.

One method of argument that your opponents may use is *argument from analogy.* The use of analogy infers that a certain fact known to be true of A is more likely to be true of B if B resembles A in certain essential characteristics or conditions.[3] Lincoln was an acknowledged master of the use of analogy. For example, as the Civil War progressed, some critics urged a change of commanders. Lincoln replied to this criticism by saying he thought it would be poor policy to change horses while crossing a stream.

When some people complained that the war was moving too slowly, this is how he responded:

> *Gentlemen, I want you to suppose a case for a moment. Suppose that all the property you were worth was in gold, and you had put it in the hands of Blondin, the famous rope-walker, to carry across the Niagara Falls on a tight rope. Would you shake the rope while he was passing over it, or keep shouting to him, "Blondin, stoop a little more! Go a little faster!"*
>
> *No, I am sure you would not. You would hold your breath as well as your tongue, and keep your hand off until he was safely over. Now, the government is in the same situation. It is carrying an immense weight across a stormy ocean. Untold treasures are in its hands. It is doing the best it can. Don't badger it! Just keep still, and it will get you safely over.*

Analogy must be used convincingly to be effective, otherwise it can fall on its face, be exposed as untrue or worthless. There's an example of this in the debate on Drug Prohibition highlighted in chapter 4. At one point in the debate, Ira Glasser, executive director of the American Civil Liberties Union, speaking for the affirmative (that drug prohibition has failed) compared the current war on drugs to the prohibition against alcohol in the 1920s, an era that became known as "The Roaring Twenties." In making his analogy, he declared:

We have spent twenty times more in this year on drug law enforcement than we spent in the late '60s when the war on drugs began. And despite all that money, despite all that growth, everyone now agrees that there is no way to keep drugs from entering this country. So what we're doing with the criminal law now is punishing the user. That's fine. Illegal drug use is down, but no more so than alcohol use or cigarette use. And we did that without prohibition.

Meanwhile consider the harm caused by prohibition. Murder rates are soaring in all of our cities. Murder rates, which went down steeply after alcohol prohibition ended [in 1933, having gone into effect in 1920 by means of an amendment to the U.S. Constitution], began to climb steeply when the war on drugs began. And innocent bystanders are being killed in epidemic proportions. Children are dying, some in their cribs, because they get in the way of stray bullets. Those people are dying, and they're dying today. Disease is spreading. In Liverpool, England, where clean needles are available [for drug addicts, free of charge], less than one percent of drug addicts carry the AIDS virus. In New York City, where you and I live, sixty percent [carry the AIDS virus]. Meanwhile, we're enriching criminals beyond belief. Drug prohibition is a government price-support system for criminal organizations. That's the legacy of drug prohibition: disease and death for innocent people and untold riches for criminals. Enough is enough.

An attempt to debunk Glasser's analogy was made by Dr. Harold Voth, a psychiatrist formerly with the Menninger Clinic and a retired rear admiral who helped the U.S. Navy with its anti-drug program. Speaking for the negative team, Dr. Voth countered:

I, of course, believe very vehemently and very strongly that prohibition is one of the key factors in controlling this terrible epidemic that's sweeping through our country. The concept is fine. The problem is we've not really made it truly operational. We have not really declared a war on drugs. We've used the word "war" on drugs, but we have not used the techniques of war. And if we really did that, I think we could win it or we would make an enormous contribution to the winning of this terrible epidemic that's sweeping through the nation.

Other nations that have liberalized the use of drugs have reversed themselves. China once had free access to opium. I think about 25 million Chinese got hooked on opium. It took them fifty years to solve that problem, but they did it, and they did it through very strict, prohibitive techniques. Japan, Sweden, Spain, and I understand more recently even Italy tried liberalizing the use of marijuana, and they quickly reversed themselves because the use went up.

I was part of the Navy program. In the late '70s about forty-seven percent of our sailors and marines, the first five enlisted grades, were using drugs. Within one year that was reduced over fifty percent, and within a year-and-a-half it was down to ten percent. I understand now it's down around five percent or below. Prohibition does work if you work at it consistently and effectively.

When your opponents use one or more analogies in their arguments, you may be able to quash them by proving one of the following:[4]

1. The details of comparison and contrast are not essential to the question at issue.
2. The points of difference outweigh the points of likeness.
3. The conclusion reached by the analogy can be discredited by other kinds of proof.
4. The fact known to be true of the analogous case is less likely to be true of the case in question.
5. The alleged facts on which the analogy is based are false.

EXPOSING ERRORS IN REASONING

A good debater on the negative side will always be on the alert for *errors in reasoning*, ready to expose them both in his or her constructive speech and in the rebuttal. When you have made a thorough preparation for a debate, you know what arguments will probably be used by the affirmative side. Knowing this, you can anticipate what arguments your opponents will try to stress. As you listen to your opponents' constructive speeches you can quickly make notes on what arguments are used and be prepared to answer them by pointing out errors in reasoning.

Errors in reasoning are known as *fallacies*. There are two basic types of fallacy.[5] One type of fallacy results from reasoning that is unclear in proving what caused certain conditions to exist. Another type of fallacy can result from reasoning that fails to prove that certain conditions will have a particular result.

You can expose fallacies by (1) proving that something else caused the conditions to exist, or (2) proving that the causes named by your opponents could not have produced, or are not solely responsible for, a particular situation. With either method you accomplish an important objective by casting doubt on the soundness of your opponents' arguments.

Here's how John Silber, president of Boston University and a member of the affirmative team in the 1991 debate on freedom of thought on U.S. campuses, exposed the fallacy expressed by some feminists that only women can speak for women:

> *I am a frequent observer of arguments in which female speakers claim that they cannot be understood by males, that only a person who is female could understand the position of women. A person who holds that point of view claims for herself a transcendence that is then denied the male. If she knows so much about what males cannot understand, then why does she suppose that the male might not be able to transcend his limits to understand her?*
>
> *A perfect example, I think, is Shakespeare. Shakespeare certainly understood his female characters extremely well, and I think we see examples of our capacity to know other people of other races and of other religions and of other sexes without any great difficulty at all. That difficulty, I think, is manufactured.*

An example of how it can be disproved that an alleged cause produced a certain effect can be seen in a hypothetical murder trial. The prosecuting attorney tries to prove that the defendant committed the murder, but unless the prosecutor has the facts to prove it, the defendant, even though guilty, may go free.

In the absence of conclusive evidence, the defense attorney, on the other hand, tries to prove that his client either had no motive to commit the murder or, if a motive was present, that there was not sufficient opportunity. The defense may also be able to prove that someone else had an even stronger motive.

SHOWING THE ABSURDITY OF YOUR OPPONENTS' ARGUMENT

Some of your opponents' arguments may appear to be so ridiculous, so poorly reasoned, that you will be able to use the *reductio ad absurdum* technique.[6] *Reductio ad absurdum* is a Latin expression which means "to reduce to absurdity." This is a technique in which an argument is disproved by showing the absurdity of its conclusion.

Here are two examples. A lawyer, perhaps in a moment of spite, once asserted in court that a corporation could not make an oral contract because a corporation has no tongue. The judge was quick to reduce this argument to absurdity by declaring, "Then, according to your own argument, a corporation could not make a written contract because it has no hand."

A more serious example relates to the controversy over slavery in the eighteenth and nineteenth centuries. Some people were opposed to the idea of freedom for black slaves and other subjugated people because they were unprepared to accept the responsibilities of freedom. Edmund Burke, the eighteenth-century British statesman and philosopher, and one of the most intelligent politicians of his day, had this answer:

> Many politicians of our time are in the habit of laying it down as a self-evident proposition that no people ought to be free till they are fit to use their freedom. The maxim is worthy of the fool in the old story who resolved not to go into the water until he had learned how to swim. If men are to wait for liberty until they become wise and good in slavery, they may indeed wait forever.

THE NEGATIVE REBUTTAL

Some of the basic tools that can be used to good effect in an affirmative rebuttal speech can work just as well for the negative side. Two fundamentals that apply, no matter which side you are on, are perceptive thinking and reasoning, and a thorough knowledge of both sides of the question. You must use these basic tools to your advantage in your constructive speech and in your rebuttal. They are especially important in making your rebuttal effective. Keep in mind that your rebuttal is your last opportunity to convince the judge that your side has the stronger and more convincing arguments.[7]

The notes you take when the affirmative side makes its constructive speeches should be your guide. Be on the lookout for flaws in their arguments. Be ready to challenge any opinions expressed that are not based on reliable facts. Also be on the lookout for any *inconsistencies* in their arguments. In his debates with Douglas, Lincoln was able to challenge Douglas's arguments on more than one occasion by exposing inconsistencies, as in the following example.

During his debates with Lincoln in 1859, Senator

Douglas maintained that the people of a territory had the lawful right to exclude slavery within its limits, in spite of the Dred Scott Decision of the U.S. Supreme Court. Lincoln exposed the inconsistency of Douglas's argument by declaring:

> The Dred Scott Decision expressly gives every citizen of the United States a right to carry his slaves into the United States Territories. And now there was some inconsistency in saying that the decision was right, and saying, too, that the people of the Territory could lawfully drive slavery out again. When all the trash, the words, the collateral matter, was cleared away from it—all the chaff fanned out of it—it was a bare absurdity: no less than that a thing may be lawfully driven away from where it has a lawful right to be.

Here again is where your perceptive thinking and reasoning will come into play. If you realize that some of your arguments lack the strength to be convincing, do not pursue them in your rebuttal. Where your arguments are strongest, however, reemphasize them as strongly as possible. Emphasis can be a very effective debating tool. In this final thrust, you should expose the weakness of the affirmative's arguments as tellingly as possible, and at the same time, pursue your most convincing lines of attack.

A good example of emphasizing the strong arguments on one side of a proposition and attempting to expose an opponent's weakness can be seen in the exchange of rebuttals in the 1991 debate on whether or not drug prohibition has failed. Representative Charles Rangel, chairman of the House Select Committee on Narcotics, spoke for the negative side, and William F.

Buckley, Jr., editor-at-large of the conservative *National Review*, spoke for the affirmative.

Declared Rangel:

What we're going to have to say is that we're going to stick with this fight until we turn it around, until we can have a drug-free community, a drug-free workplace, and we can regain the leadership that we rightfully deserve. The answer is not in doctors' offices, it's not in the pews of churches, it's not in our jail cells. But we have to know one thing: that as long as people find themselves not in schools, without jobs, without training, without hope, yes, they'll look for something to ease the pain.

Some unscrupulous doctors will give them legal drugs. To say that we should just open it up so that everyone that feels pain should not have hope and should be discouraged and think they should depend on dope rather than trying to get their lives together would just be to give up on these people, on these communities, and on this country.

What would this world be like if every time we saw that there was a problem and every time we saw it wasn't working the way that we would want it to work, we would just say, "Let's legalize it and move on to something else." You wouldn't want it for your kids. I don't want it for my children and my grandchildren.

Buckley underscored his response by using the following quote from a surprising source:

"The desire for crack runs wild and takes madness into its service. Any opinions or desires

TIPS ON DESTROYING YOUR OPPONENTS' ARGUMENTS

- Be thorough enough in your research so you will have a clear understanding of both sides of the issue. You can then challenge any arguments expressed that are not based on reliable facts.
- Respond to all of your opponents' arguments with strong arguments of your own, based on clear logic and convincing evidence.
- Use only the most persuasive evidence to support your case.
- Be careful not to claim more than the evidence justifies. Exaggeration will weaken your arguments.
- Point out holes in your opponents' arguments. When they use analogies, quash them if you can by proving they are weak, unconvincing, or inappropriate to the question at issue.
- Expose errors in reasoning and arguments by showing the absurdity of their conclusions. Expose fallacies by proving (1) that something else caused the conditions to exist, or (2) that the causes named by your opponents could not have produced or are not solely responsible for a particular situation.
- Use emphasis and repetition to drive home your strongest arguments.

with a decent reputation and any feeling of shame still left are killed or thrown out until all discipline is swept away and madness usurps its place. When crack has absolute control of a man's mind, life is a round of orgies and sex, so that whatever income he has will soon be expended.

"Next, of course, he will start borrowing and drawing upon his capital. When he comes to the end of his father's and mother's resources, he will start by burgling a house and holding someone up at night or go to clean out a church. Meanwhile the older beliefs about honor and dishonor which he was brought up to accept as right will be overcome by others once held in restraint."

Those words were written by [the ancient Greek philosopher] Plato, and the word "crack" was stuck in for "passion." So the phenomenon that we are accosted with is a phenomenon that has beset civilization ever since it escaped from Paradise. We're not suggesting that we have a cure for the problem. Far from it. What we are insisting on is that we have laid out the documentation that shows that millions of Americans are terrorized every single day in pursuit of a program which, by Mr. Rangel's own definition, is getting us nowhere. We should, under the circumstances, not only mobilize our resources to denounce the use of drugs, to expose the dangers inherent in the use of drugs, but to liberate our society from the incidental damage that a misbegotten program has bequeathed us.

EIGHT

LISTENING TO YOUR OPPONENT AND RESPONDING EFFECTIVELY

No matter how strong your constructive speech may be, you will have a different kind of challenge when you make your rebuttal. To be successful you must listen carefully to all the opposing arguments and be fully prepared to answer them, especially those that question your credibility and thereby threaten your position on the proposition.[1] You must make a strong response, a response that is convincing and persuasive, in order to be judged the winner.

As always, the key is preparation, being aware of all the main points on both sides of the issue and having the strongest possible evidence to support your views. You can probably anticipate most of the arguments your opponents will use, but be prepared for surprises.

Through research you'll come to know your own strong and weak points. You will also discover and make notes on your opponents' strong and weak arguments. But you must respond to what you read and make it your own. This will happen when you select the evidence and arguments to use in your constructive speech and in preparation for your rebuttal.

As a skillful debater, you may have enough rebuttal material to talk for an hour, even though you know there may be only five minutes allowed. The great advantage is that you lessen the chances of being surprised by your opponents' line of attack and, guided by notes taken when your opponents are speaking, you have the material you need to respond effectively.[2] A skillful debater will also carefully group evidence and material in anticipation of what the opponents' main lines of attack may be.

AN UNSUSPECTED ARGUMENT

But what if you are surprised by an unsuspected argument or unfamiliar evidence? You won't have time to collect new evidence for your rebuttal. The only alternative left is to decide as quickly as you can just what bearing it has on the proposition and what its relation is to your own arguments. You will also have to use your judgment in deciding whether it's worth answering. If it is, then you will have to find evidence and arguments strong enough to rebut it successfully.[3]

A slipshod approach to your opponents' rebuttal can only be disastrous. If you know the main issues, the major arguments on both sides of the question, there is no need to jot down a lot of miscellaneous points made by your opponents that are not worth answering.[4] Some of your opponents' points may be concerned with minor issues, not the main issues, and therefore not worth arguing. Don't waste time and thought on these. Answer all of your opponents' challenges and arguments so you won't run the risk of losing points, but stick to the main issues and drive your own points home.

If you are well prepared you have already laid the groundwork for an effective rebuttal. You will have your briefs (topic sheets) or note cards, each headed by a separate topic describing the evidence or argument. It may also be helpful to number each card or brief con-

The 1992 Presidential candidates engaged in a number of different styles of debates. Left: The candidates during a formal debate. Above: A lighter moment during their "town-hall meeting" debate, which featured audience questions.

secutively, then make a numbered list of topics for quick reference. This will save time. The time allowed for you to prepare for your rebuttal will be limited. It might be ten or fifteen minutes, and you should be prepared to work as quickly as you can.[5]

GETTING OFF THE TRACK

There may be times when some of the statements made by your opponents are so illogical or so far from the point that they appear stupid and pointless. It may be tempting to come up with a statement in your rebuttal that will embarrass your opponents by holding them up to ridicule, but don't do it. That can get you off the track and is known as *introducing personalities* into a debate.

Calling your opponents "stupid," for example, won't win you any points with the judge.[6] Point out the errors that have been made by your opponents, but don't dwell on them. Stick to the main line of your argument and drive your own points home.

UNITY AND EMPHASIS

Your best attack, both in your constructive speech and in your rebuttal, is a *unified attack*. What this means is that all of your arguments and evidence should fit together as a whole. Introducing personalities is not the only way to get yourself off the track and destroy a unified approach. Another pitfall to avoid is relying too heavily on statements of authority, anecdotes, and personal comments.

If you have prepared your constructive speech well, all of your evidence and arguments will fit together. They have one unified purpose: to reinforce your stand on the proposition.

Use the same approach in your rebuttal, making

the best possible use of the time allowed. Here is where you can make skillful use of emphasis by repeating your strongest arguments. It may not hurt your case if the judge forgets some of your less important points, the subordinate issues. Stress your major arguments. Emphasize them through skillful repetition so that they will not be forgotten.

In his debates with Lincoln, Douglas asserted again and again "the right of the people of a state to settle the question of slavery for themselves," and demanded "obedience to the decision of the highest tribunal in the land, the Supreme Court." Similarly, Lincoln turned again and again to his main argument that "a house divided against itself cannot stand; this government cannot endure permanently half-slave and half-free."

Also, Lincoln reminded his audiences again and again that Douglas had said, "I do not care whether slavery is voted up or down." When you are repeating your main arguments, try to express them in phrases so clear, exact, and striking that they will bear frequent repetition.

USING A FLOWSHEET

Your single most valuable tool in taking notes during a debate while your opponents are speaking is the flowsheet. A flowsheet accomplishes two important objectives: (1) it saves time by helping you organize your notes and comments for use in your rebuttal, and (2) it helps make your notes as complete as possible because they will be grouped under specific arguments.[7] A legal-size notepad is recommended for use as a flowsheet. It should be divided into the following four columns:

Affirmative Case	Negative Case	Affirmative Counterarguments	Negative Counterarguments

If you are on the affirmative side, in Column 1 outline your team's case as it will be presented in your constructive speeches, but in abbreviated form. Use short phrases, sometimes only a few words or even one word will be sufficient, as long as it provides enough of an indication of the argument or evidence.

Use the same approach in Column 2, where you indicate the main points and evidence presented by the negative team in its constructive speeches. This, of course, must be done quickly as you listen to your opponents. Here again, a thorough knowledge of your opponents' side of the issue as well as your own, reinforced with notes on sheets or cards, will prove valuable.

In Column 3 list the arguments and evidence that your side will be using in your rebuttals. If you have numbered or coded your note cards or sheets you can just use the number or code, to save time. Use Column 4 to indicate the counter-arguments used by the negative side in its rebuttal.

Use the flowsheet in the same way if you are on the negative side. Whichever team you are on, you will be under a certain amount of pressure to get as much information down as possible in a limited amount of time.

It will also help if you are able to develop some kind of *shorthand* so that you can get down as much information as you think you will need for an effective response. When you take notes in class you probably use some version of shorthand for the same reason. Some words are not written down at all because you know where to fill them in. This would probably be true of certain articles, adjectives, conjunctions, and helping verbs.

If you don't have a shorthand system already at hand, ask your debate coach for guidelines and examples of how you can develop a system you can use to good effect during a debate. Whatever system you develop, make sure your notes are legible and accurate.

FLOWING: AFFIRMATIVE VS. NEGATIVE

Some debaters refer to the use of flowsheets as "flowing." Whatever term is used to describe this process, the use of a flowsheet to highlight the main arguments of both sides, in both the constructive speeches and the rebuttals, can mean the difference between losing or winning a debate. A good example of the effective use of flowsheets can be seen in the results of the international debate held February 26, 1992, at Bates College in Lewiston, Maine.[8] The debate centered on the proposition: "Resolved: The Atomic Bombing of Hiroshima Was Justified."

The bombing of Hiroshima, Japan, on August 6, 1945, was followed three days later by the dropping of a second and more powerful atomic bomb on Nagasaki, which led almost immediately to Japan's unconditional surrender to the United States and its Allies, thus ending World War II.

Each team included one American student and one from Japan. On the affirmative team, representing the U.S. government's point of view, were Sarah Watson of Bates College and Hajime Kawada of Waseda University. Opposing were Dan Schwager of Bates and Tomoyuki Uda of Sophia University. The debate was conducted in English, both Japanese students being fluent in that language. The format used was parliamentary debate, an Americanized version of the type of debate used in the British Parliament.

Another interesting aspect of this type of debate is that it is open to the public, with the outcome decided not by a judge but by a vote of the audience. In this particular debate round both the affirmative and negative sides argued their cases so effectively that the audience of sixty persons was almost equally divided as to who won the debate. However, negative team members Dan Schwager and Tomoyuki Uda edged out the affirmative team by five votes, scoring 32 votes to their opponents' 27.

The main thrusts of the affirmative's arguments in their constructive speeches and rebuttals included the following:

1. The atomic bombing of Hiroshima saved the lives of thousands of American and Japanese soldiers by bringing a prompt end to the war.

FLOWSHEET FOR PROPOSITION: "RESOLVED:

Affirmative Case	Negative Case
atomic bombing saved thousands of soldiers' lives, Japanese and American	Hiroshima civilian target
no weapons of war are "reasonable" or "humane"	thousands of innocent lives destroyed
holding out for uncond. surrender best hope for lasting peace	Japan ready to discuss cond. surrender May 1945
no conclusive evidence Japan would have accepted cond. surrender	US insisted on uncond. surrender
Hiroshima was military target, site of military HQ	A-bomb not conventional—radiation poisoning—should not have been used
Japan had no intention of surrendering until 2nd A-bomb dropped	Pres. Truman's estimate of military casualties if Japan invaded was inflated
	dropping A-bomb not justified—all other reasonable alternatives not considered

---

2. (In response to the argument that the atomic bomb was an unreasonable, horrible weapon, not like the conventional weapons then being used) Are there any "reasonable" weapons? Bombing is a part of war.
3. The United States and its Allies were right in holding out for Japan's unconditional surrender because it supported the cause of lasting peace.
4. There is no evidence that a conditional surrender would have been accepted by either Japan or the United States and its Allies.
5. Hiroshima was chosen because it was a mili-

THE ATOMIC BOMBING OF HIROSHIMA WAS JUSTIFIED."

Affirmative Counterarguments	Negative Counterarguments
U.S. justified in wanting to end war as soon as possible	bomb could have been dropped on strictly military target, saving thousands of civilian lives
Japanese needed psychological shock to convince them	use of A-bomb not military necessity. Japan losing war, many Japanese leaders ready to negotiate
Japanese trained to fight to the death—e.g., Okinawa, Iwo Jima	
Japanese people told they were winning war	personal accounts of horrible suffering and death of women, children, old people
only way to save American lives was to end war	Russian declaration of war on Japan would have led to surrender
	Japanese emperor wanted to end war

tary target and not because of its large civilian population.

6. Japan had no intention of surrendering, conditionally or unconditionally. It did not capitulate until the second atomic bomb was dropped on Nagasaki.

The negative team countered with these main arguments:

1. Hiroshima was a civilian target, not a military target. Thousands of innocent lives were destroyed and thousands of others suffered the lifelong effects of radiation poisoning.
2. It wasn't necessary to drop the atomic bomb to make Japan surrender. The Japanese were ready to discuss terms of a conditional surrender in May 1945, but the United States and its Allies stubbornly insisted on unconditional surrender.
3. The atomic bomb was different from conventional bombs and should not have been used because the radiation poisoning it caused lasted for years.
4. U.S. President Harry S. Truman was wrong in saying that an invasion of Japan (as an alternative to using the atomic bomb) would have resulted in the deaths of 500,000 soldiers. The more likely figure is 40,000, which is far fewer than the thousands of people killed in Hiroshima.
5. Dropping the atomic bomb on Hiroshima was not justified because all of the reasonable alternatives had not been considered.

All of the above arguments are referenced or suggested in the sample flowsheet.

NINE

METHODS OF JUDGING

Whenever you participate in a debate you will be judged according to a strict set of guidelines set forth for that particular type of debate. These will include use of a point system in evaluating your performance in each aspect of the debate.

Two popular types of high school debating are the Policy Debate, also known as the Oregon Style or Team Debate, with two members each on the affirmative and negative sides, and the Lincoln-Douglas Debate in which there is only one person debating each side of the question.

JUDGING POLICY DEBATE

The Policy Debate features eight-minute constructive speeches by each team member in which they must present their most convincing arguments and evidence. The affirmative team is expected to present a workable plan that meets present needs and prove that it can solve the problem highlighted in the resolution. It must also meet the criterions of each of the four stock issues: *Significance, Inherency, Solvency,* and *Advantages.* If the affirmative team fails in meeting the criterion of only one stock issue, it will automatically lose the debate. This is a unique feature of Policy Debate.[1]

After each constructive speech the speaker stays at the podium while a member of the opposing team is allowed three minutes to ask questions. This is called "cross-examination," and the purpose is twofold: to obtain information about your opponent's sources of information and at the same time attempt to find flaws in his or her arguments. It is also an opportunity to clarify whatever is not yet clear about the opponent's arguments and evidence. When you are the cross-examiner, however, you should not express any conclusions. These should be saved for your rebuttal speech.

For the rebuttal speeches each team member is allowed four minutes. The rules of this type of debate prohibit the introduction of any new arguments during a rebuttal speech. However, new evidence and new interpretations of arguments that have already been introduced are allowed. The negative team's rebuttal should challenge the affirmative's presentation of the stock issues one at a time and in the order in which the affirmative team presented them. This makes it easier for the judge to evaluate the rebuttal.

Judges in Policy Debates, as in all types of debates, expect any unfamiliar terms used by a debater to be clearly explained or defined. Each argument used should be well organized and clearly presented. "Spreading" (speaking very rapidly) is discouraged and may count against you because the judge may not listen carefully to what he cannot "flow" or take notes on.[2]

During each constructive speech and rebuttal the judge will take notes outlining the major points of each speaker. He or she will also keep close watch on the time, signaling by use of fingers the number of minutes remaining. When time has run out the judge will call out,

"Time." This will bring an immediate cut off to the speech. Oftentimes in a debate tournament five minutes will be allowed per team for "preparation time." This time allotment is to be used between speeches, giving you added opportunity to get your notes in order for your response. When a team exceeds the time allowed for preparation, the extra time is deducted from the time allowed for their response.[3]

SPEAKER POINTS

The win/loss decision in Policy Debate is based on which team was most successful in supporting their arguments. Each speaker is ranked from 1 to 4, with the best speaker ranked number 1. Speaker points are assessed to reflect how well each debater argued, with five points possible in each of six categories: analysis, reasoning, evidence, organization, refutation, and delivery. These categories are defined as follows:

Analysis: identifying and arguing the major issues in the debate, with points also considered for effectiveness of cross-examination.

Reasoning: effectively creating clash by arguing and presenting one side of the debate, extending an argument, turning the opponents' arguments against them, exposing faulty logic, and extending an argument based on a major item of evidence.

Evidence: quality of sources, applying the evidence to a specific argument, using evidence to support major arguments, showing how well the evidence is understood.

Organization: structure of speeches, i.e., introduction, arguments, and summary; following the flow of the debate; coherency; and effective use of time.

Refutation: effectively weakening opponents' arguments, creating clash, and *addressing all arguments in the debate.*

Delivery: clarity, pronunciation, poise, gestures, eye contact, projection of personality, sentence structure, and grammar.

With 30 possible points (five points each in six categories) in this type of debate, a tally of 26 or 27 is considered a high score and 18 to 20 is considered a low score. The judge knows that it is the goal of each debater to persuade the judge that he or she has the most convincing arguments and should be judged the winner. However, in all Policy Debates the bottom line is always based on how each stock issue is handled by each team. When you are not successful in getting all possible points in one of the categories, the judge will use the comments section of the ballot to explain why points were deducted.

JUDGING THE LINCOLN-DOUGLAS DEBATE

Lincoln-Douglas Debate has several marked differences from Policy Debate. It is a one-on-one performance in which the sole proponents of the affirmative and negative sides of a resolution confront each other. There is no requirement for either side to present a workable plan as a solution to the resolution. Instead, each side must convince the judge that one value or set of values is more important than those presented by his or her opponent.[4] One example of a Lincoln-Douglas Debate topic is the following:

Resolved: A victim's deliberate use of deadly force is justified as a response to physical abuse.

In debating this and other Lincoln-Douglas Debate resolutions, the emphasis will not be on evidence but on reasoning, logic, and persuasion. As in all debates, the judge is expected to be objective. The judge must evaluate each debater on the basis of who had a better grasp of the basic premises of the debate.

The judge must also decide which debater more clearly defended his or her case and better attacked the opponent's case. Evidence is important in support of logic, reasoning, and argumentation, but the judge's evaluation will be based on how it is used rather than on how much is used.[5]

There are four sections to the Lincoln-Douglas Debate ballot, with one set for the affirmative side, the other for the negative. The first three are Case and Analysis, Support of Issues Through Evidence and Reasoning, and Delivery. In assigning points for the first two sections the judge must decide which debater's argument was more persuasive. The judge must also decide which debater communicated more effectively in supporting his or her position by using logical arguments throughout, and evidence where necessary.

Points for delivery are assigned on the basis of speaking ability. The judge will give you points according to how poised you are and how clear you are in presenting your ideas.

There are four ranges of scoring: superior, excellent, good, and average. The points in the superior range are from 47 to 50; excellent 43 to 46; good 39 to 42; and average 35 to 38. The judge's primary concern will be focused on the arguments presented by each side. Any argument, however weak, will stand unless it is successfully refuted. As in all debates, the winner will be the one who presents the most convincing arguments.

The fourth and final section of the Lincoln-Douglas Debate ballot is reserved for the judge to give reasons and summary comments for his decision.

THE CASE SUMMARY METHOD

Other methods of judging are used for other types of debate. For example, one is the *Case Summary*

THE CASE SUMMARY METHOD

Affirmative	Negative

1st Aff.

I._____

  A._____

  B._____

II._____

  A._____

  B._____

. . . etc.

2nd Aff.

I._____

. . . etc.

1st Aff. Rebuttal

I._____

. . . etc.

2nd Aff. Rebuttal

I._____

. . . etc.

1st Neg.

I._____

  A._____

  B._____

  C._____

II._____

  A._____

    1._____

. . . etc.

2nd Neg.

I._____

. . . etc.

1st Neg. Rebuttal

I._____

. . . etc.

2nd Neg. Rebuttal

I._____

. . . etc.

From *Argumentation and Debate*, by Austin J. Freeley, © 1961 by Wadsworth Publishing. Reprinted with permission.

Method, in which the judge records an outline of the case.[6] Using a sheet of paper divided vertically, the judge records the issues and evidence presented by the affirmative on one half and the negative on the other. Several sheets of paper may be needed.

Each judge will have his or her own style in making use of this sheet. Some will use different colored pencils or draw lines from one item to another. Some judges have their own symbols to indicate how the arguments develop, where the opposing arguments clash, and to record other information, such as notes on the effectiveness of delivery.

THE ISSUE SUMMARY METHOD

Another method used by some judges in formal debates is the *Issue Summary Method.*[7] This also involves sheets of paper, but in this method horizontal lines are used. Each issue is assigned a horizontal column, with Roman numerals used to identify each issue. As each issue is developed or challenged by affirmative or negative speakers, the judge indicates this by using a triple X (XXX).

The arguments of the first affirmative speaker are recorded in the column headed 1A. This speaker's rebuttal arguments are recorded in the column headed 1AR. The same system of recording is used for all of the affirmative and negative speakers, the number of speakers depending on the kind of formal debate being used.

It is worth noting that many trial judges and attorneys use a similar method as they record the progress of debate in the courtroom. Many business executives also use a similar method as an aid in weighing arguments in favor or against a corporate policy being considered.

THE ISSUE SUMMARY METHOD

Issue	1 A	1 N	2 A	2 N	1 NR	1 AR	2 NR	2 AR
I. xxx	xxx	xxx		xxx		xxx	xxx	
II. xxx	xxx	xxx	xxx					xxx
III. xxx	xxx		xxx	xxx	xxx			xxx
IV. xxx		xxx	xxx	xxx			xxx	
V. xxx			xxx	xxx		xxx	xxx	xxx
VI. xxx			xxx	xxx	xxx		xxx	xxx

From *Argumentation and Debate*, by Austin J. Freeley, © 1961 by Wadsworth Publishing. Reprinted with permission.

THE ORAL CRITIQUE

In some formal debates the judge will deliver an *oral critique*[8] based on the notes and other methods of judging used during the debate. The judge will take several minutes to review this information before making an oral critique. An effective oral critique will accomplish the following:

1. Review the progress of the debate
2. Cite examples of effective use of the principles of argumentation and debate
3. Offer suggestions for improvement
4. Cite the most important factors used in arriving at a decision
5. Announce the decision

When the decision is in your team's favor, it is good to know exactly how the judge reached this decision. If you have lost, it is also good to know why, and also how you can best improve your techniques so you will have a better chance of winning next time.

THE BALLOT

The most common form of reporting decisions in a formal debate is the ballot. One reason this is preferred is that it provides a permanent record of the event. Sometimes an oral critique is given along with presentation of the ballot. Or sometimes a judge may be asked to prepare a written critique along with the ballot. An effective ballot will provide all of the the following information:

1. Record the decision on the debate
2. Record quality-rating points on important criteria for each debater
3. Record the rank of each debater
4. For each team, provide a record of the achievements of each of the participants
5. Provide a permanent record of the results

A ballot that meets these requirements is shown on pages 90 and 91. The top portion is used for the permanent record of the school sponsoring the debate. The middle section is given to the affirmative team at the conclusion of the debate, and the bottom section is given to the negative team. These sections report on the quality of the participants' debating performance in the following areas: analysis—plan of case; knowledge and evidence; reasoning, inferences; adapting to opposing case; skill in refutation; speaking skill.

Each debater is ranked in order of excellence by placing 1, 2, 3, or 4 in the parentheses to the right of the debater's name in all three sections of the form. The number 1 indicates the most effective, 4 the least effective. However, in judging the quality of debating for each of the six phases of the debate, the numbering system used for points is: 1—poor; 2—fair; 3—good;

OFFICIAL JUDGING FORM

Classification _____ Round _____ Date _____ Judge _____

Aff. Team _____ vs. Neg. Team _____

	Rank	Points			Rank	Points
1st Aff. Speaker _____	(____)	(____)	1st Neg. Speaker _____		(____)	(____)
2nd Aff. Speaker _____	(____)	(____)	2nd Neg. Speaker _____		(____)	(____)

Team Totals (Points) _____ Aff. _____ Neg. _____

In my opinion, the more effective debating was done by the

team from _____ _____
(Name of College) (Aff. or Neg.)

_____ _____
(Signed) (Judge)

TO THE JUDGE: Please fill in the entire ballot. Please do not render a decision as a tie. The debaters will greatly appreciate it if you will write your comments on the back of the appropriate section below. These sections will be given to the teams as indicated. The above section is for our files.
Speaker's Norms: 7 or below poor; 8 to 13 fair; 14 to 19 good; 20 to 25 excellent; 26 to 30 superior.
Team Norms: 14 or below poor; 15 to 26 fair; 27 to 38 good; 39 to 50 excellent; 51 to 60 superior.

FOR THE AFFIRMATIVE TEAM

Aff. _____ vs. Neg. _____ Judge _____

I. *Quality of Debating*

NOTE: Assign to each speaker the *points* which best describe your evaluation of the quality of debating done in each of the six phases.
1 — poor; 2 — fair; 3 — good; 4 — excellent; 5 — superior.

	Affirmative		Negative	
	1. Rank (____)	2. Rank (____)	1. Rank (____)	2. Rank (____)
Analysis — plan of case				
Knowledge and Evidence				
Reasoning, inferences				
Adapting to opposing case				
Skill in refutation				
Speaking skill				

Speaker's Totals (points)

Team Totals (points)   Aff. _____   Neg. _____

II. *Rank of Debaters*

NOTE: Please rank debaters in order of their excellence by placing 1, 2, 3 ,or 4 in the parentheses to the right of the debater's name in all three sections of this form.
(1 indicated the most effective; 4 the least effective)

III. *Decision*
    The more effective debating was done by: _____

FOR THE NEGATIVE TEAM

Aff. _____ vs. Neg. _____ Judge _____

I. *Quality of Debating*

NOTE: Assign to each speaker the points which best describe your evaluation of the quality of debating done in each of the six phases.
1 — poor; 2 — fair; 3 — good; 4 — excellent; 5 — superior.

	Affirmative Rank			Negative Rank	
	1 2 3 (4 5)	1 2 3 (4 5)	1 2 3 (4 5)	1 2 3 (4 5)	1 2 3 (4 5)
Analysis — plan of case					
Knowledge and Evidence					
Reasoning, inferences					
Adapting to opposing case					
Skill in refutation					
Speaking skill					

Speaker's Totals (points)

Team Totals (points)   Aff. _____   Neg. _____

II. *Rank of Debaters*

NOTE: Please rank debaters in order of their excellence by placing 1, 2, 3 ,or 4 in the parentheses to the right of the debater's name in all three sections of this form.
(1 indicated the most effective; 4 the least effective)

III. *Decision*
    The more effective debating was done by: _____

From *Argumentation and Debate*, by Austin J. Freeley, © 1961 by Wadsworth Publishing. Reprinted with permission.

4—excellent; and 5—superior. The team with the highest number of points is judged the winner.

DIRECT-CLASH DEBATING BALLOT

Another type of ballot used in formal debating is the Direct-Clash Debating ballot, shown on page 93. This ballot is based on how the opposing teams, affirmative and negative, handle direct clashes of opinion. In other words,[9] how effectively they are able to handle specific arguments, those offered as evidence by one side and opposed by the other.

OFFICIAL AUDIENCE
SHIFT-OF-OPINION BALLOT

INSTRUCTIONS TO THE AUDIENCE:

The debaters will appreciate your interest and cooperation if you will, *both before and after the debate*, indicate on this ballot your personal opinion on the proposition of the debate.

The proposition is: "Resolved: That [the proposition of the debate is stated here]."

BEFORE THE DEBATE FILL OUT THIS SIDE	*AFTER* THE DEBATE FILL OUT THIS SIDE
(Check one)	(Check one)
_____ I agree with the proposition.	_____ I agree with the proposition.
_____ I am undecided.	_____ I am undecided.
_____ I am opposed to the proposition.	_____ I am opposed to the proposition.

From *Argumentation and Debate*, by Austin J. Freeley, © 1961 by Wadsworth Publishing. Reprinted with permission.

Still another ballot, this one for use by the audience, is called the Official Audience Shift-of-Opinion Ballot. This can be used to determine how effective one team

OFFICIAL JUDGING FORM FOR DIRECT-CLASH DEBATES

Classification _____ Round _____ Date _____ Judge _____

Aff. Team _____ vs. Neg. Team _____

No. of clashes won: Aff. _____ Neg. _____

Therefore, the winner of this debate was the _____
(Aff. or Neg.)

team from: _____ Signed: _____
(Name of College)   (Judge)

FOR THE AFFIRMATIVE TEAM

Aff. _____ vs. Neg. _____ Judge _____

Clash 1 _____ _____

Clash 2 _____ _____

Clash 3 _____ _____

Clash 4 _____ _____

Clash 5 _____ _____

No. of clashes won: Aff._____ Neg._____

Decision won by: _____

FOR THE NEGATIVE TEAM

Aff. _____ vs. Neg. _____ Judge_____

Clash 1 _____ _____

Clash 2 _____ _____

Clash 3 _____ _____

Clash 4 _____ _____

Clash 5 _____ _____

No. of clashes won: Aff._____ Neg._____

Decision won by: _____

From *Argumentation and Debate*, by Austin J. Freeley, © 1961 by Wadsworth Publishing. Reprinted with permission.

or the other is in confirming or changing the audience's opinion about the proposition being debated. It also adds an extra challenge to those involved in a debate to win the audience, as well as the judge, to their side. It is a good test of effective conviction and persuasion.

TEN

TYPES OF DEBATE

All types of debate have many characteristics in common. There are always two opposing sides, with one in favor of the proposition or resolution, the other opposed to it. Each side begins with constructive speeches in which the main arguments for or against the proposition are presented. Both sides use flow-sheets to note important arguments and evidence presented by both sides as the debate progresses. And each side has an opportunity to make rebuttal speeches as their final persuasive effort.

Each segment of the debate must be presented within strict time limits. In deciding which person or team is the most persuasive the judge will be using essentially the same criteria.

STANDARD DEBATING

In general, all debates can be said to have the following three elements in common: (1) both sides must have an equal number of speakers; (2) both sides must have an equal amount of time; and (3) the affirmative side must speak first and last. The standard type of debating, the one most widely used in the United States, is structured as follows:

95

First affirmative speech	10 minutes
First negative speech	10 minutes
Second affirmative speech	10 minutes
Second negative speech	10 minutes
First negative rebuttal	5 minutes
First affirmative rebuttal	5 minutes
Second negative rebuttal	5 minutes
Second affirmative rebuttal	5 minutes

Policy Debate

As in Standard Debate, there are two team members on each side in Policy Debate. However, there the similarity ends. Policy Debate is not just concerned with affirmative and negative points of view. The challenge for the affirmative side in this type of debate is to present a plan that will prove certain stock issues forming the basis for the resolution being debated. If the negative team can prove the affirmative side wrong on just one of the stock issues, they will win the debate.

After each constructive speech in which arguments are used to make a case, there is a cross-examination by an opposing team member. The speaker stays at the podium or lectern while a member of the opposing team asks questions, with three minutes allowed for this purpose. The goal of the questioner is twofold: to gain information and to try to make the speaker admit flaws in his or her arguments.[1]

The rebuttal speeches are only half as long as the constructive speeches, four minutes compared to eight minutes, and have special restrictions. Speakers may not introduce any new arguments; however they are permitted to introduce new evidence and new interpretations or critiques of arguments that have already been introduced.[2] Here's the format for Policy Debate:

| First affirmative constructive speech | eight minutes |
| Cross-examination by second negative speaker | three minutes |

First negative constructive speech	eight minutes
Cross-examination by first affirmative speaker	three minutes
Second affirmative constructive speech	eight minutes
Cross-examination by first negative speaker	three minutes
Second negative constructive speech	eight minutes
Cross-examination by second affirmative speaker	three minutes
Rebuttal by first negative speaker	four minutes
Rebuttal by first affirmative speaker	four minutes
Rebuttal by second negative speaker	four minutes
Rebuttal by second affirmative speaker	four minutes

Note: In his or her constructive speech the second negative speaker has an obligation to present new arguments and evidence in direct response to the first affirmative speaker's constructive speech. This speaker should also state, for the benefit of the judge, that his or her partner will respond to the second affirmative's constructive speech in rebuttal.

Another point to keep in mind is that in Policy Debate the first affirmative speaker has the most difficult task because his or her rebuttal speech must be given after twelve minutes of negative arguments. All of their arguments must be responded to in only four minutes, the time allowed for the rebuttal speech.[3]

LINCOLN-DOUGLAS DEBATE

The Lincoln-Douglas Debate, although different in that it is value-centered and pits one person against the other, has one element in common with Policy Debate in that each participant has an opportunity to cross-examine the opponent.

You begin your affirmative constructive speech by stating what the resolution is, defining key words in the resolution, and then build a case in which the values stated in the resolution are upheld. You build your case by presenting arguments that support your point of view. When the speech ends you are cross-examined by your opponent.

When used effectively, cross-examination gives a debater the opportunity to clarify points in the opponent's position and to expose factual errors. An attempt should also be made to obtain damaging admissions and to set up arguments that can be used in your rebuttal speech.

As recommended by the National Forensic League, questions should be brief and the answers short and specific. However, answers cannot be held to a simple "yes" or "no." Also, the questioner should not be allowed to comment on the answers.[4] Throughout the cross-examination both debaters should look at the judge and not at each other.

If you are the negative, you need to give definitions only if you think yours are "superior." You must present your contentions, and must also address the affirmative's case to fulfill the basic premise of any debate, which is clash.[5] When you finish your negative constructive speech, you will also be subject to cross-examination in the same manner as stated above.

When giving their rebuttal speeches, both affirmative and negative debaters should reiterate and strengthen their cases, and at the same time address and point out weaknesses in the opponent's case. In doing this, however, no new issues may be introduced. The format for Lincoln-Douglas Debate is as follows:

Affirmative constructive speech six minutes
Negative cross-examination three minutes
Negative constructive speech seven minutes

Affirmative cross-examination	three minutes
First affirmative rebuttal	four minutes
Negative rebuttal	six minutes
Second affirmative rebuttal	three minutes

PARLIAMENTARY DEBATE

Parliamentary Debate is an Americanized version of the type of debate conducted in Great Britain's Houses of Parliament in which spokesmen for the Government (the affirmative side) in favor of a particular proposition present their case and are challenged by representatives of the Opposition (the negative side). There are two members on each team, and each one makes a constructive speech. However, only the first negative speaker and the first affirmative speaker make rebuttal speeches.[6]

Parliamentary Debate is conducted before an audience. After all the constructive speeches have been made, members of the audience selected at random make floor speeches of about one minute's duration. These can be in support of either side. Also permitted are cross-bench speeches, a form of floor speech in which disagreement with both sides is expressed. Usually about six floor speeches are permitted, the number depending on the time set aside for this phase of the debate. The format for Parliamentary Debate is as follows:

First affirmative constructive speech	eight minutes
First negative constructive speech	eight minutes
Second affirmative constructive speech	eight minutes
Second negative constructive speech	eight minutes
Six one-minute floor speeches	six minutes
First negative rebuttal speech	four minutes

First affirmative rebuttal speech   four minutes
Voting by audience (show of hands to
    determine winner)

DIRECT CLASH DEBATE

Another interesting variation in formal debating is the Direct Clash Debate.[7] In this type of debating the judge takes an active role in the conduct of the debate. In the version designed for two-person teams, the following format is used.

Definition and Analysis.
1. The first affirmative defines terms and outlines the affirmative team's basic position on the proposition, stating the issues that the affirmative team wants to debate (5 minutes).
2. The first negative either accepts or rejects the affirmative's definition and analysis and the proposed issues to be debated. The negative has the option of proposing additional issues to be debated. If a counter plan is proposed, it must be presented as an issue at this time (5 minutes).
3. The judge may rule on the issues at this time.

First Clash.
1. The second affirmative presents a single issue that he or she believes vital to the affirmative's case (4 minutes).
2. The second negative attempts to disprove the preceding speech (3 minutes).
3. The first affirmative reestablishes the second affirmative's argument (3 minutes).
4. The first negative then attempts to disprove the argument (3 minutes).

5. When this clash ends, the judge records the winner on his or her ballot and announces the decision.

Second Clash.
1. The second negative presents a single issue (4 minutes).
2. The second affirmative attempts to disprove the argument (3 minutes).
3. The first negative reestablishes the issue (3 minutes).
4. The first affirmative now attempts to disprove the argument (3 minutes).
5. The judge records the winner on his or her ballot and announces the decision.

Third Clash.
This clash follows the same pattern as the others, but this time the first affirmative presents a single issue. The judge announces his or her decision and whether another clash is needed.

Fourth Clash.
Again the same pattern is followed, with the first negative initiating the issue.

Fifth Clash.
Again the same pattern is followed, with the second affirmative initiating the issue.

In this style of formal debating, when each person or team member clashes on a specific issue, only that particular issue may be argued, not the entire proposition. Also, after the definition and analysis stage, the judge has the option of playing an active role in the conduct of the debate.

However, if the judge believes that the definition of

terms and statement of basic positions have been expressed clearly and convincingly, the debate may be allowed to continue without direction from him or her. Sometimes, however, there may be a strong disagreement over terms. When that happens the judge may rule that the first clash must deal with this problem.

When the statement of basic positions of both or either teams is not clear, the judge may take charge by stating the issues that should be debated. He or she will also determine the order in which they will be debated. The judge may also take charge when a speaker evades a point in one of the clashes or answers so inadequately that the position of the speaker's team on that issue is destroyed. When that happens the judge may stop the clash.

This type of debate is usually limited to five clashes, but under the rules of Direct-Clash Debate the debate continues until one team has won three clashes. This means there must be at least three clashes but no more than five.

THE HECKLING DEBATE

The Heckling Debate[8] follows the pattern of legislative debate as it is practiced in state legislatures or in the House of Representatives or Senate. This is how it is structured:

First affirmative	10 minutes
Heckling by first negative	
First negative	10 minutes
Heckling by second affirmative	
Second affirmative	10 minutes
Heckling by second negative	
Second negative	10 minutes
Heckling by first affirmative	
First negative rebuttal	5 minutes
Heckling by first affirmative	

First affirmative rebuttal	5 minutes
Heckling by second negative	
Second negative rebuttal	5 minutes
Heckling by second affirmative	
Second affirmative rebuttal	5 minutes
Heckling by first negative	

In a Heckling Debate, speakers on both sides of the question can be interrupted by members of the opposing team. This must be done formally, however, by asking, "Will the speaker yield for a question?" The speaker, of course, has no choice. He or she must yield. However, the question must be short and must be directly related to the argument or evidence the speaker is discussing.

During the constructive speech (opening statement) the heckler may interrupt the speaker four times. Interruption may occur any time after the third minute of the speech and before the eighth minute. During the rebuttal speech, the heckler may interrupt twice—any time after the first minute of the rebuttal and prior to the fourth minute.

In some ways the Heckling Debate is similar to the cross-examination style of debating used by law students. The responses to the questions asked by the hecklers are designed to be used later by the hecklers, either to advance their own case or challenge their opponents' case. However, the judge will penalize a heckler if he or she asks questions that are too long or irrelevant. Also, this type of debate requires very careful timing. The timekeeper in this style of debate is therefore instructed to announce, at the designated time, "Heckling may begin" or "Heckling must cease."

THE DEBATE-FORUM

The Debate-Forum,[9] like the Lincoln-Douglas Debate, lends itself well to television and is often used during political campaigns of national importance, such as the presidential election campaign. The most common format is that of the standard debate discussed at the beginning of this chapter. This is followed by a "forum" period, during which time members of the audience are invited to address questions to the debaters.

In the Debate-Forum the constructive speeches or opening statements are shorter, and may be only six minutes long. The rebuttal speeches may be limited to three minutes. The time allowed will depend on the number of debaters.

By shortening the time for constructive and rebuttal speeches, and allowing twenty minutes for questions from the audience, this type of debate can be scheduled for an hour, which is well-adapted to television requirements.

A chairperson or moderator will be designated to oversee the debate and, in particular, the forum portion. It will be his or her responsibility to prevent a few questioners from monopolizing the forum period. The chairperson must also discourage speeches from the floor that are disguised as questions. Wordy or vague questions, or those difficult to hear, must be restated so that the entire audience can hear them. It is also the chairperson's responsibility to make sure the debating process and forum period move along at a good pace and stick to the topic.

DEBATING IN YOUR STATE

If you and other classmates are interested in organizing a debate team or finding out about educational debates scheduled in your state, contact the president of the state Forensic Association. This person will be able to provide you with information about both state and national debates.

Your state's Forensic Association will also be able

to provide you and your instructor with details on how a debate team can be organized, and how it can meet Forensic Association standards. Another good source of information about debates and debating teams is your state's School Principals Association.

APPENDIX ONE

*I*DEAS FOR DEBATE TOPICS

This section contains eighty suggested debate topics arranged in twenty subject areas. Most of the topics were drawn from two major research sources for high school debaters: the *Opposing Viewpoints* series published by Greenhaven Press and *SIRS*, the Social Issues Resources Series, one or both of which may be found in your school library. Another excellent research source are transcripts of the Firing Line Debates produced by the Southern Educational Communications Association. To obtain a catalog write to Southern Educational Communications Association, Inc., P.O. Box 5966, Columbia, South Carolina 29250.

Subject Areas

Abortion	Free Speech
Affirmative Action	The Homeless
America's Future	Homosexuality
Criminal Justice	Male/Female Roles
Death and Dying	The Military
Drug Use	Pornography
The Elderly	Poverty
Ethics in Government	Protecting the Environment

Sexual Harassment   Social Justice
Sexuality   Violence in America

Abortion

RESOLVED:

That Pro-Life Extremist Tactics Should Be Condemned
That Men Should Take Part in Abortion Decisions
That Abortion Is Immoral
That the Unwanted Child Is Justification for Abortion

Affirmative Action

RESOLVED:

That Affirmative Action Has Improved Race Relations
That Affirmative Action Is Needed to Break Down Stereotypes That Divide America
That Affirmative Action Is a Tool of Oppression for Blacks and Other Minorities, Not an Opportunity
That Preferential Treatment for Blacks and Other Minorities Contributes to Racial Tensions in Any Environment in Which It Exists

America's Future

RESOLVED:

That America Is in Decline as a World Power
That America's Educational System Is Second Class
That Capitalism Is and Will Continue to Be the Most Important Source of America's Traditional Values

That America Should Work to Strengthen the United Nations as the Dominant Power in the World

Criminal Justice

RESOLVED:

That the Death Penalty Should Be Abolished

That the Criminal Justice Sentencing Process Is Ineffective and a Burden on the Taxpayer

That Crime Victims Are Too Often Ignored Under the Present Judicial System

That Criminal Law Should Be Strengthened and Punishment Increased as a Deterrent to Crime

Death and Dying

RESOLVED:

That Families Should Be Encouraged to Ask Doctors to Remove Life-Support Systems When a Family Member Is Terminally Ill

That Assisted Suicide Is Morally Acceptable

That Life Is Precious to All of Us and Should Be Sustained at All Costs

That Everyone Has the Right to End His Life No Matter What the Consequences

Drug Use

RESOLVED:

That All Anti-Drug Laws Should Be Abolished

That the War on Drugs Should Be Intensified

That the War on Drugs Is a Waste of Taxpayers' Money

That Marijuana Should Be Legalized

The Elderly

RESOLVED:

That Social Security Payments Should Be Made Only to Those Who Need Them to Survive

That Medicare Funding for Nursing Home Care Should Be Increased

That Age Seventy Should Be the Recommended Age for Retirement and Eligibility for Social Security Retirement Benefits

That Families Should Be Given Financial Incentives to Care for Elderly Relatives

Ethics in Government

RESOLVED:

That Criminal Penalties Should Be Enacted to Punish Those Who Lie and Mislead Voters During Political Campaigns

That American Foreign Policy Should Be Based on Political Morality

That the U.S. Park Service's First Concern Should Be Protection of Wildlife and the Environment in all Public Lands It Oversees

That the Government Does Not Have the Right to Legislate Morality

Free Speech

RESOLVED:

That School Administrators and Teachers Do Not Have the Right to Censor Student Publications

That Laws Should Be Enacted to Prohibit Obscene Music, Movies, Videos, and All Pornographic Publications

That the Government Should Not Fund or Support Ex-
hibits of Obscene Works of Art
That National Security Always Justifies Censorship

The Homeless

RESOLVED:

That No U.S. Citizen Should Be Allowed to Go Home-
less Regardless of the Cause
That the Policy of De-Institutionalization of the Mentally
Handicapped Is a Major Cause of Homelessness
That Legislation Should Be Enacted to Provide Job
Training and Shelter for the Homeless
That Homelessness Is Destroying the Moral Fabric of
American Society

Homosexuality

RESOLVED:

That Homosexuals Deserve the Same Respect and
Protection Under the Law as Other Minorities
That Homosexuality Should Be Discouraged Both Mor-
ally and Legally
That Any Teenager Who Is Troubled by Homosexual
Feelings Should Seek Psychological Help to Rein-
force His/Her Heterosexuality
That All Gay Teenagers Should be Respected by Their
Peers

Male/Female Roles

RESOLVED:

That the Feminist Movement Has Forced Men to Become Second-Class Citizens

That Ardent Feminists Do Not Make Good Wives and
    Mothers
That Male Bonding Groups Are Detrimental to Good
    Male/Female Relations
That Traditional Sex Roles Are Too Restrictive

The Military

RESOLVED:

That the U.S. Military Presence in Europe Is a Needless
    Expense
That Gays in the Military Should Have Separate Living
    Quarters and Not Be Allowed to Mix Socially with
    Heterosexuals
That Legislation Should Be Enacted and Enforced to
    Prevent Outrageous Waste in Military Expenditures
That Women in the Military Should Be Trained for
    Combat

Pornography

RESOLVED:

That Pornography Violates Women's Civil Rights
That Pornography Is a Moral, Not a Civil Rights Issue
That the First Amendment Does Not Protect Pornog-
    raphy
That Pornography Should Not Be Censored

Poverty

RESOLVED:

That the Capitalist System Causes Poverty
That Sexism Keeps Women Poor

That Welfare Programs Victimize the Poor
That Poverty in America Is Not a Serious Problem

Protecting the Environment

RESOLVED:

That Brazil and All Other Countries Should Be Prohibited from Destroying Rain Forests
That the Greenhouse Effect Is a Myth
That Only Government Intervention Can Protect the Environment
That the Use of Alternative Fuels Should Be Encouraged to Reduce Air Pollution

Sexual Harassment

RESOLVED:

That Anita Hill's Sexual Harassment Testimony Against Clarence Thomas Was Unconvincing
That Existing Laws Provide Sufficient Protection from Sexual Harassment
That Better Laws Are Needed to Protect Both Men and Women from Sexual Harassment
That Better School Policies Are Needed to Protect Both Female and Male Students from Sexual Harassment by Staff, Teachers, and Their Peers

Sexuality

RESOLVED:

That Schools Should Play the Major Role in Sex Education
That Parents Should Bear the Primary Responsibility for Sex Education
That Teenagers Should Have the Same Sexual Freedom Enjoyed by Adults

That Conception Prevention Should Be Taught in Junior High and High School to Reduce Teenage Pregnancies

Social Justice

RESOLVED:

That Minorities Should Not Receive Special Economic Privileges

That All Illegal Immigrants Should Be Allowed to Qualify for U.S. Citizenship

That Hispanics and Other Immigrants from Non-English Speaking Countries Have a Right to Bilingual Education

That the Exploitation of Women Is Exaggerated

Violence in America

RESOLVED:

That Stronger Gun Laws Will Not Significantly Reduce Violence in America

That Stronger Gun Laws Are Needed to Reduce Violence in the Home and on the Street

That Violence Is An Acceptable Way of Life for Americans

That Violence Is Promoted, Encouraged, and Glorified in Movies and on Television

ANNUAL NATIONAL DEBATE COMPETITIONS

Annual Debate Tournament of the Catholic Forensic League. Open to contestants from all public and private schools. Held at various sites in the United States. For information write to Richard Gaudette, Secretary-Treasurer, Catholic Forensic League, Natick High School, Natick, MA 01760.

California Invitational, National High School Forensics Tournament, University of California at Berkeley. Held annually during Presidents' Day weekend in February for Policy Debate teams, Lincoln-Douglas Debaters, and individual speaking events. The California Invitational is a Kentucky Tournament of Champions (see below) qualifier in both Policy Debate and Lincoln-Douglas Debate. Invitation and entry packet available by writing to Tournament Director, California Invitational, University of California at Berkeley, 102 Sproul Hall, Berkeley, CA 94720, or FAX requests to 510-799-2755.

Harvard Debate Tournament. Held in February at Harvard University, Cambridge, Massachusetts. For information write to Dallas Perkins, Harvard Debate

Tournament, Quincy House, Harvard University, Cambridge, MA. 02138

National Speech and Debate Tournament. Sponsored by the National Forensic League, held in June at various host high schools in the United States. For information write to the National Forensic League, P.O. Box 38, Ripon, Wisconsin, 54971. Telephone 414-748-6206.

Tournament of Champions. Held annually in May at the University of Kentucky in Lexington, Sponsored by the University of Kentucky Debate Association. For information write to the Director of Debate, University of Kentucky, Lexington, KY 40506.

ƧOURCE NOTES

CHAPTER 1   THE JOYS AND CHALLENGES
OF DEBATING

1. William Trufant Foster, author of *Argumentation and Debating* (Boston: Houghton Mifflin, 1932).

CHAPTER 2   HOW DEBATERS ARE JUDGED

1. Notes from interview with Scott Murray, student debater, Scarborough High School, Scarborough, Maine, April 4, 1992.
2. Notes from interview with Robert J. Hoy, debate coach, Brunswick High School, Brunswick, Maine, April 8, 1992.
3. Ibid.

CHAPTER 3   PREPARING FOR DEBATE

1. William Trufant Foster, *Argumentation and Debating* (Boston: Houghton Mifflin, 1932) p. 203 and ff.
2. Notes from interview with Robert J. Hoy.
3. Foster, p. 59 and ff.
4. Ibid., p. 77 and ff.

5. Freeley, Austin J., *Argumentation and Debate* (Belmont, California: Wadsworth Publishing Co., 1981) p. 306.
6. Ibid., p. 306.
7. Foster, pp. 142–143.

CHAPTER 4   METHODS OF ARGUMENT

1. Carney, James D., and Scheer, Richard K., *Fundamentals of Logic* (New York: Macmillan Publishing Co., Inc., 1974) p. 3 and ff.
2. Ibid., p. 9 and ff.
3. Foster, p. 77 and ff.
4. Ibid., p. 269 and ff.

CHAPTER 5   MAKING YOUR DELIVERY EFFECTIVE

1. Foster, pp. 315–318.
2. Gulley, Halbert E., and Biddle, Phillips R., *Essentials of Debate* (New York: Holt, Rinehart and Winston, Inc., 1972) pp. 75–81.
3. Foster, pp. 319–320.
4. Ibid., pp. 321–322.
5. Ibid., pp. 268–269.
6. Notes from interview with Scott Murray.
7. Foster, p. 272.
8. Ibid., p. 273.

CHAPTER 6   TAKING THE AFFIRMATIVE SIDE

1. Notes from interview with Robert J. Hoy.
2. Notes from interview with Scott Murray.
3. Foster, pp. 77–78.
4. Ibid., pp. 189–190.
5. Ibid., pp. 142–143.

CHAPTER 7 HOW THE NEGATIVE ATTACKS

1. Notes from interview with citizen judge Nathan Dennis, Mt. Ararat High School, Topsham, Maine, April 4, 1922.
2. Foster, pp. 77 and ff.
3. Ibid., pp. 109–111.
4. Ibid., p. 147.
5. Ibid., pp. 154–155.
6. Ibid., p. 177.
7. Notes from interview with Scott Murray.

CHAPTER 8 LISTENING TO YOUR OPPONENT AND RESPONDING EFFECTIVELY

1. Notes from interview with Scott Murray.
2. Foster, p. 304 and ff.
3. Notes from interview with Robert J. Hoy.
4. Ibid.
5. Notes from interview with Scott Murray.
6. Foster, pp. 311–312.
7. Notes from interview with Robert J. Hoy.
8. Notes from presentations of Sarah Watson and Dan Schwager, Bates College, Lewiston, Maine: Hajime Kawada, Waseda University, Japan; and Tomoyuki Uda, Sophia University, Japan, at international debate at Bates College, February 26, 1992.

CHAPTER 9 METHODS OF JUDGING

1. Notes from interview with Nathan Dennis.
2. Ibid.
3. Ibid.
4. Ibid.
5. Ibid.
6. Freeley, p. 284.
7. Ibid., pp. 284–286.

8. Ibid., p. 285.
9. Ibid., pp. 309–310.

CHAPTER 10   TYPES OF DEBATE

1. Notes from interview with Robert J. Hoy.
2. Ibid.
3. Notes from interview with Scott Murray.
4. Notes from interview with Nathan Dennis.
5. Notes from interview with Robert J. Hoy.
6. Notes from interview with student debater Dan Schwager, Bates College, Lewiston, Maine, February 26, 1992.
7. Freeley, pp. 309–310.
8. Ibid., pp. 311–312.
9. Ibid., pp. 313–314.

$\mathscr{G}$LOSSARY

Advantages. A stock issue in Policy Debate. In response to the resolution, the affirmative team must prove it has a workable plan with desirable advantages.

Affirmative team. The team that argues in favor of the proposition.

Analyzing the proposition. Studying all the arguments and evidence to find the main issues in favor of or against the proposition.

Argumentation. To show the likelihood, through arguments, examples, evidence, and persuasion that a given proposition is true or false. A synonym for debate.

Argument from analogy. A technique in which a debater infers that a certain fact known to be true of A, is more likely to be true of B, if B resembles A in certain essential characteristics or conditions.

Arguments. Facts, authoritative statements, other evidence and reasoning in favor of or against the proposition.

Ballot. In formal debate the most common form of reporting decisions, with points and ratings assigned by the judge to each affirmative and negative team member, as well as to the team as a whole. The top portion is used for the permanent record of the school sponsoring the debate, the middle portion is given to the affirmative team, and the bottom portion to the negative team.

Case. A set of reasons, arguments, supporting facts, and other evidence presented in favor of or against the proposition.

Case Summary Method. A procedure in which a judge records an outline of the cases presented by the affirmative and negative teams, using sheets of paper divided by a vertical line. The issues, arguments, and evidence presented by the affirmative team are recorded on one side, and by the negative team on the other side.

Counter-argument. An opposing argument put forward by one team against an argument presented by the opposing team.

Debate-Forum. Standard debate followed by a forum period in which members of the audience are invited to address questions to the debaters. A chairperson or moderator oversees both the debate and the forum portion.

Deductive reasoning. A method of logic in which you begin with a generalization and thereby reach a specific conclusion.

Direct-Clash Debate. A form of debate in which affirmative and negative teams clash on specific issues until one team has won three clashes and is declared the winner. The judge may take an active role in this type of formal debate.

Errors in reasoning. Faulty logic, incomplete or unsubstantiated evidence, and fallacies that weaken or destroy a debater's arguments.

Evidence. Facts, examples, statements of authority, and other information used by a debater to strengthen his or her arguments to prove or disprove the proposition being debated.

Fallacies. Errors in reasoning or arguments that are unsuccessful in proving (1) what caused certain conditions to exist or (2) that certain conditions will have a particular result.

Flowsheet. One of the tools of debate used to record arguments, counter-arguments, and evidence put forth by a debating team and its opponents. By using shorthand, a team is able to record a great deal of information in a limited amount of time for possible use in rebuttal speeches.

Formal Educational Debate. A form of debate that includes the following requirements: (1) both sides must have an equal number of speakers; (2) both sides must have an equal amount of time.

Heckling Debate. A type of formal debate designed to simulate legislative debate as practiced in the state legislature or in the House of Representatives or Senate. Speakers on both sides of the proposition can be questioned by members of the opposing team during their speeches, with limits set for the number of questions, and the time in which they can be asked.

Inconsistencies. Elements of reasoning and argument that are unsound because they ignore, omit, misinterpret, or withhold important evidence or facts.

Inductive reasoning. A method of logic in which you begin with specific facts or examples and thereby reach a generalization or conclusion.

Inherency. A Policy Debate stock issue. The affirmative team must convince the judge that the problem stated in the resolution is central or inherent to the present system.

Introducing personalities. Attacking your opponents personally. Not recommended.

Issue Summary Method. A judging procedure in which the judge uses sheets of paper with columns indicating the issues raised, which speakers raise them, and when they are challenged by the opposition.

Lincoln-Douglas Debate. A two-person formal debate named in honor of the famous duo who used this form to debate the slavery issue in 1858 and 1859.

Logic. That part of argumentation concerned with the reasoning process.

Main issues. The major evidence used by affirmative and negative teams to prove or disprove the proposition.

Negative team. The team that argues against the proposition.

Opening statement. A constructive speech that each side uses to begin the debate.

Oral critique. A procedure in which the judge criticizes the debate orally, based on notes and other methods of judging she or he has used during the debate.

Parliamentary Debate. An Americanized version of the type of debate conducted in Great Britain's Houses of Parliament, with two members on each team, one team representing the Government's point of view (affirmative), the other the Opposition (negative). It is conducted before an audience, some of whom are permitted to make one-minute floor speeches. The audience votes to decide the winner.

Policy Debate. A form of team debate in which the challenge of the affirmative team is to prove certain stock issues that form the basis of the resolution being debated. After each constructive speech, the speaker is cross-examined by one of his opponents.

Prima facie case. A term used to describe the first affirmative constructive speech in Policy Debate in which evidence is presented that establishes a fact or raises a presumption of fact. *Prima facie* means "at first sight" or "before closer inspection."

Proposition. The statement on which a debate is based.

Rebuttal. The response to your opponents' arguments and counter-arguments.

Reductio ad absurdum. A technique used to reduce an opponent's arguments to absurdity.

Shorthand. A system of taking notes in which unnecessary words are omitted and some necessary words are shortened or abbreviated. It may include symbols, acronyms (words formed from the initial letters of a name, e.g., UN = United Nations), and other word substitution techniques. To be effective it must be legible and accurate.

Significance. A Policy Debate stock issue. The affirmative team must convince the judge that there is a significant problem with the present system.

Solvency. A Policy Debate stock issue. The affirmative team must prove that the plan they propose will work to solve the problem as described in the resolution.

Subordinate issues. Issues important to the arguments presented but secondary to the main issues.

Topicality. One of the stock issues in Policy Debate. The affirmative team must respond to the problem exactly as worded in the resolution.

Unified attack. A method of attack or presentation in which all of a debater's arguments and evidence fit together as a whole.

Weight of evidence. The sum total of all the evidence presented to prove or disprove the proposition.

$\mathscr{F}$OR FURTHER READING

Barnet, Sylvan, ed. *Current Issues and Enduring Questions: Methods and Models of Argument*, 2d edition. New York: Bedford Books (St. Martin's Press), 1989.

Branham, Robert James. *Debate and Critical Analysis: The Harmony of Conflict.* Lawrence Erlbaum Associates, Hillside, New Jersey, 1991.

Eisenberg, Abne M. and Ilardo, Joseph A. *Argument: A Guide to Formal and Informal Debate*, 2d edition. New York: Prentice-Hall Press, Speech Communication Series, 1980.

Freeley, Austin J. *Argumentation and Debate* 7th edition. Belmont, California: Wadsworth Publishing Co., 1989.

Hensley, Dana and Prentice, Diana. *Mastering Competitive Debate*, 3d edition. Caldwell, Ind.: Clark Publishing, 1987.

Herrick, James A. *Critical Thinking: The Analysis of Argument*, Scottsdale, AZ: Gorsuch Scarisbrick, 1991.

Makau, Josina M. *Reasoning and Communication: Thinking Critically about Arguments.* Belmont, Calif.: Wadsworth Publishing, 1990.

Zarefsky, David. *Lincoln, Douglas and Slavery: In the Crucible of Public Debate.* Chicago: University of Chicago Press, 1990

INDEX